ISLAND VOICES

ISLAND VOICES

Fiona MacDonald

•

Foreword by
Iain Crichton Smith

CANONGATE PRESS

To my mother and father
with love

First published in 1992 by Carrick Media.
First published in paperback in 1994 by
Canongate Press Ltd,
14 Frederick Street,
Edinburgh EH2 2HB.

British Cataloguing-in-Publication Data
A catalogue record for this book is available on request
from the British Library.

ISBN 0 86241 469 5

Set by The Format Factory, Mansfield
Printed and bound in Great Britain by
Bookcraft Ltd, Midsomer Norton, Avon

CONTENTS

FOREWORD

A book of this kind depends, I suppose, on how interesting the interviewees are, and how honest and direct they are. It also depends on the width of the spectrum of opinions, and lives, that are illuminated.

On both these counts, I found the book enlightening.

Not only are there the indigenous inhabitants of the islands – men, women, girls, a school child, bachelors etc. – who talk sometimes about the past – the Highland Clearances, the history of the Gaelic language, religion, the beauty and freedom of the landscape – but also the incomers, who come generally from England, and relate their physical and psychological struggles in adapting to a way of life which must have been quite alien, at least to some of them. The incomers in this book are not critical about their new home, in general. Some try to learn Gaelic, some cope with sheep shearing and so on. Some are artists, some are photographers, some become live-wires in the community. Some are seeking solitude, some are sick of the city, some are searching for community. They all realise that in the words of one of the interviewees, "you have to be quite strong to survive."

Some of the indigenous ones are gloomy about the future of Gaelic, others are optimistic. One passes on the history of her little world to her grand-nieces and nephews. Many praise the Gaelic songs and poetry, and some do not find pleasure in the new Gaelic TV programmes.

I was particularly impressed by two or three people in the book, and they were the ones who had very strong principles and beliefs. Tex Geddes is clearly a born rebel, with very fixed convictions. He stayed on in Soay, Skye, in spite of a concerted campaign by the authorities to remove him. He is clear-headed, unsentimental, brusque. "You know this bed and breakfast thing? I think it's the most degrading profession there ever was."

Ena Parkin is another "character", strong, determined, fascinating. She led a teenage rebellion from Tarbert Hostel against Sabbatarian church parades. She worked in private service for Jews in London who had bullet-proof glass against terrorists. She says that she "never gave a reference to anyone unless they gave one to me." She was born in Berneray and has returned to it.

But I think the wisest and most wide-ranging interview is that with Canon MacQueen, South Uist. He tells us of his days beachcombing, and of his love of glass, old bottles which he picks up along the shore. His vision of the priesthood is 24 hours a day service. He seems a most humane man, who has thought deeply of what being an islander means. Thus though a Hebridean can be the life and soul of a party, in his deepest being "he is not really a party man." He says that "English was created for chemists and doctors to write prescriptions" but lacks the beauty and harmony of Gaelic. He tells of how the Hebridean is able to cope with death, as if it were an ordinary event, which it is. This is a quality of the Hebridean which is commented on by others as well. Whereas in cities death is a secret fact, in the Hebrides it is handled calmly and with dignity.

I think that anyone who wants to know about the "islander" has only to read this analysis.

We are at the moment at the heart of a very profound struggle in the islands. Will they survive as centres of Gaelic culture or will they simply become "ordinary" islands on the periphery of so-called civilisation? Will they be irretrievably changed by "incomers" and new values? Is, for instance, the "keeping of Sunday" necessary to this survival? All these are questions to which one feels answers are imminent. None of the "incomers" here is hostile to the culture which they are entering. They in their turn seem thoughtful enough people, unwilling to be associated with their brasher brothers.

This book will contribute to a continuing dialogue about the worth and persistence of Hebridean values. No-one knows where the pendulum will eventually rest. "Our time has no favourite suburb," wrote Auden: and to maintain one's "world" one has to work very hard.

IAIN CRICHTON SMITH   August 1992

AUTHOR'S NOTE

Motivated by a deep, lifelong affection for the island of Tiree, I set out in this book to capture the changing character of the Hebrides. Locals and incomers, young and old welcomed me into their homes and allowed me to question them, and I extend to all of them my grateful thanks for this privilege. I visited some to discuss a specific subject; with others the conversation meandered through a range of topics.

Help was also given by the late John Campbell of Lewis and Ayr; Dr. James Hunter in Skye; Charles Kennedy, MP; Ian McCormack, editor, West Highland Free Press; Donald Macdonald of North Uist and Glasgow; Rev. Norman Maciver in Harris; Donnie Maclean in Lewis; Ivor Morrison in Lewis; Irene Underwood in Coll; Rev. Adrian Varwell in Benbecula; and by many others.

The interviews took place between July 1990 and October 1991 on 13 Hebridean islands. Although a tape recorder was used, each interview has been edited and some grammatical errors have been corrected. However, every attempt has been made to maintain a conversational style.

Finally, I am grateful to Kenneth Roy of Carrick Media for the opportunity to write this book and for his encouragement.

FIONA MacDONALD   August 1992

And then a queer thought came to her there in the drooked fields, that nothing endured at all, nothing but the land she passed across, tossed and turned and perpetually changed below the hands of the crofter folk...

Lewis Grassic Gibbon
Sunset Song

Canon Angus John MacQueen

Bornish, South Uist

Canon Angus John MacQueen was born and brought up in Eochar at the north end of South Uist. He trained for the priesthood at Blairs College in Aberdeen, and has served in Dunoon, Barra (twice), Mallaig, Eriskay, Ballachulish, Rothesay, and Arran (where he opened the first Catholic church since the Reformation). He is now back on his native island where he has a small parish of about 300 souls.

In Barra he had a boat to fish for lobsters, in Ballachulish he caught prawns, and now he has a sheep farm with 56 breeding ewes.

I absolutely love being outdoors. My hobby all my life has been beachcombing. And anyone who is a beachcomber has a particular philosophy. First of all, you're not interfering in anybody else's life. You're well out of everybody's way. And, if you're a thinker, it's a marvellous opportunity for thinking, and a marvellous opportunity if you're a bard for composing, or if you're a preacher, for building up thoughts for sermons. And the next thing is that it's recreational because of the fantastic amount of variety in beachcombing. The weather is one factor, the state of the tide another, the state of the wind and the tide combined onto the shore is another. And then, always there is the wealth of the sea coming in.

Now, we live in the days of plastics of course. I spend a lot of time reading plastic, and cartons of milk from Denmark and Canada and Holland and Sweden, and God knows whatnot.

There's also fishing material coming in, and dead sea birds as well as live ones offshore. There are whales, there are sharks, there are dolphins, there are occasional interesting fish like John Dorys. All kinds of things come ashore, especially after the big gales.

It's an irresponsible kind of pastime – selfish, I suppose, in many ways – because it's escapist. Purely escapist. Except, from my viewpoint, if I'm at home the telephone will be ringing or people like yourself will be arriving at the door. But when I'm along the shore people can never keep up with me. They've tried. And they've tried to make conversation with me walking along the shore. I remember a man who was trying to film me had a terrible time; but then, he was from London so it didn't really... Anyway, that's my pastime and the beautiful thing about beachcombing is that you collect everything and you just sift it later on. You find yourself dragging things along. On the window behind you there is a whole selection of the flotsam and jetsam of the ocean: glass fishing-balls, shells, bottles, all kinds of things.

I have a great friend who is now very old – Peggy Angus, the artist – who had a house on Barra. And she and I used to walk the shore together. Now, she learned folk art on the island of Bali, where you don't have to work for your living because there is food in the trees all round you but every day everybody creates something beautiful and you give it to a friend at the end of the day or you buy a new friend with it at the end of the day. So we would go for a walk along the beach and we'd find a piece of cork, a bashed tin, the leg of a chair, shells and things, and we would sit and she would create a picture out of that. Once she found a tin and with a pebble she managed to make a lovely picture of St. Brendan preaching to the seals in relief on it.

I am madly in love with glass – any kind of glass. So if I find a bottle, I'll be particularly interested and I'll hold it up against the light and see what it does for me. You'll see lots of bottles in my windows in various tints and colours and, for me, they're very important. Useless of course. Not worth money or anything – one never looks for that. I would never dream of going out with one of these detectors to find coins and things. That is not my idea of beachcombing. My idea of beachcombing is always to be amazed at the wonder of God's creation, to find God's bounty in literally everything – the Celtic view of the bounty of God and the goodness of God through creation.

And, of course, the bonus at the end of the day is that you have nothing between yourself and the horizon. So you will see a sunset and you will see the birds on their way back to the cliffs, and you'll tell the time by the type of birds that are hugging the shore on their way back, and you will see the night arriving again. And then you'll walk back and you'll meet people who'll be out doing their chores here, there and everywhere, and you'll pass the time of day with them and talk to them about cabbages and kings and then you'll come home and you'll make a peat fire and you'll sit down and do a bit of reading and if you're hungry you'll make yourself a bit of food. That's my other hobby of course – cooking, seafood cooking.

So that's what I enjoy – beachcombing and being outdoors, and looking, observing, and filling a storehouse of knowledge, of joy, of love, through creation.

In contrast to their Presbyterian neighbours, South Uist, Eriskay, Barra and Vatersay are predominantly Catholic. Is there a Celtic dimension to their Catholicism?

Oh yes. Of course there is. To begin with, we presume that God doesn't speak English, or doesn't understand English.

Gaelic is not a speaking language, it's a singing language. The word *can* [say] comes from the Latin word *cantare* – to sing. Whereas English is a prosaic language. English was created for chemists and doctors to write prescriptions. It's not a language, it's a means of communication. But Gaelic is a singing language – with a small vocabulary but with each word loaded with meaning.

Therefore, we have this advantage of Gaelic in the Celtic world.

And we have, of course, kept all the old Celtic customs. For instance, we have just finished the festival of St. Michael when we celebrated the harvest and we made the Michaelmas cake with the first fruits of the harvest. And going back to pre-Christian times, all the beautiful things from then have been kept in the process of adopting Catholicism; many have been married into the practice of religion. So we keep the feast of Bride at the beginning of spring to coincide with the birth of nature.

All these things are terribly important to us and the Celtic side of spirituality is very attractive to islanders because we are a solitary people. Hebrideans are solitary people because of the nature of our work. Yesterday, here in Bornish, I met a couple of lads wandering down with knapsacks on their backs – they should have been in school of course – to break tangles. It was early and they would be on their own until 6 o'clock at night with their own thoughts, breaking tangles all day long. Now, city people tell me the most terrifying thing is the thought of getting to know themselves. But Hebrideans know themselves from their earliest days. They will go off to the hill or off to the shore or off somewhere and spend hours on their own. And it's when you're on your own that you get to know yourself and what you're all about.

So, although Hebrideans are the heart and soul of the party when they're at a party, they're not party people. They're happiest on their own – solitary, wandering about, doing their own thing. Whether you're after sheep or after cows, or whatever it is you're doing, you're on your own. We are solitary people, like so many of the world's folk – people from the high sierras, people from Lapland, Africans, South Americans. It's only city people who depend on each other for living. They've got to have bodies all round them. They've got to know that there's someone round the corner, whereas a Hebridean could live on his own on rocks – or on Rockall for that matter – in the middle of nowhere.

So, that is the philosophy of mind of the Celt. That is the first thing you learn. You are at peace in your own mind. You are you and whether you like yourself or not, you have got to respect yourself and love yourself because you are a special creation of God's and you're so different from anybody else that ever lived. And you treat others with the same great respect.

The Celt was always a strong-willed person who was able to live in communion with nature, with creation. If the Israelites hadn't composed the psalms, the Hebridean would have because he is completely in tune with the psalms, and in tune with creation; in tune with spring, summer, autumn, winter, various moods; in tune with the spring tide or the neap tide; in tune with the moon and the sun and the stars and the wonders of creation.

The prayer of the Hebrideans is repetitive – repetitive in the nicest possible way. They repeat the same prayer – whether it's the Lord's Prayer or the Hail Mary, or whatever they're doing – and they're quite prepared to do it for hours and hours on end. That's why you'll find old Hebrideans sitting beside the fire when the eve of their lives has arrived saying the rosary, or saying ave Marias from morning till night. They're quite happy to be doing it. It's their life and they're relaxed about it. God said if you want anything you should ask for it, and keep on asking for it. And they keep asking. The Celtic mind is to keep asking because you have a childlike trust in a bountiful God. I mean, when you're an island person and you're hemmed in by nothing but an imaginary line called the horizon, you are utterly dependent on the bounty of God's creation.

What led him to the priesthood?

I'm sure it was this love, this great awe, of God and his creation. And this basic thing in Christianity of being available to others permanently – 24 hours a day – that always appealed to me.

I became a priest in the days when we still had the barter system. There was no money when I was a boy, after the First World War. You went to a shop with eggs and used them in lieu of money or you went with rabbits or whatever you had.

The world wasn't an attractive item after the First World War. Men had come back to the land fit for heroes to find that the ones that had stayed alive were just a bit superfluous. There was no new land. There had been great promises that land would be available to the islanders coming back. But it was still the same system where the oldest son could stay around until the father who had the croft died, and then take it over. The rest had to face the wide world.

So it wasn't an attractive world to be in after the First World War and the high ideals of my schoolmaster, who is still alive and lives in the south of England, gave us one great thing – a love for learning. I don't understand children today saying, "I hate school." We were given a great thirst for learning by someone who was very enlightened – a real Celt. He was from Barra. He would enthuse us with geography, he would enthuse us with history, although, of course, unlike the Irish, Hebrideans were never taught history. We were taught innocent history that wouldn't upset the mind or the heart or make you hate people. They never told us about the clearances. We spent our time learning about the battles of Crecy and Agincourt – things that wouldn't hurt a fly and meant nothing to anybody. It was a silly sort of history we were taught. But it was innocuous. Utterly innocuous. Meaningless and innocuous.

One exulted over the battle of Bannockburn and the battle of Stirling Bridge and we knew about the Union of the Crowns and things like that. But I think there was no harm done to the young mind by not revealing everything to it. You can see the danger of what they did in Ireland when they taught local history in the schools. A great deal of the hatred that is happening in Ireland is because young people are so aware of the wrongs and rights of life in their own history. We were saved from that.

We only heard about these things from arguments at home. My father being a bard, our house was full every night. All the men gathered. The first man would light the pipe and the pipe would go round – it would be an insult to light two pipes, one pipe went round all night – and when it emptied the next man would fill it, and so on. First of all, the conversation would be about the happenings of the day – whether anybody had composed any songs or whatever. And, of course, it was sufficiently close to the First World War that people still lived that. They were still in the trenches mentally. They were still suffering these terrible, terrible months and weeks they had spent in the trenches. Then they would move on to talk about the evictions and the clearances. I was born in 1923, that was the year people went to Canada and it wasn't an eviction but it was near enough because there was no living or life in the island. They had to emigrate.

So the men would sit and argue back and forward and when the argument would get too hot my mother would chase the children to bed. So we did hear about these things – but never in school. At school you were mentally cosseted from the hurt of life.

So anyway, in school we did our geography and history. And we had a great love of English. Gaelic was proscribed. When I went to school I didn't know a single word of English but I had to learn it in order to learn that two and two make four. We had to learn the three Rs through the medium of English. By law. By British law. So we had to capture the English language and we fell madly in love with it because of the way it was taught then. We were taught grammar and being bilingual one immediately absorbed grammar syntax. And we had great spelling-bees and learned how to spell things like "ecstasy" and so on and, by the time you were eight, there wasn't a word in the shorter dictionary you couldn't spell and many of them you actually understood.

And this schoolmaster put high ideals in front of us. This is the whole thing. He had very high ideals about whatever you wanted to do, and the priesthood – giving your life for the service of God – was the very highest thing you could do. To make yourself available 24 hours a day, especially in a celibate state, was something so unreachable that it seemed to be particularly attractive. But, equally, he put the same sort of ideals before those who wanted to do something different. For example, when he talked about the merchant navy, he would talk about being a captain. We were taught that Hebrideans had it in them to lead, to be the top, to be the best in everything they did.

•••

Of course, your home was a house of prayer. When I would be playing with my Protestant pal and it came to Bible reading time, I would go and sit quietly in his house until they finished so that I would get a piece and jam. He would be in my place and we would be playing around and we would stop for rosary or night prayers or whatever, and my father would lead them, and my Protestant pal would be there throughout that. And it was the most natural thing in the world that families were praying families.

I don't think anything ever added to the strength of the faith that I got at my mother's and father's knees. Your faith was so deeply rooted in you from your very earliest days, that I don't think it ever needed to be strengthened.

As Hebridean Christians you met everything head-on. I remember when I was four or five a neighbour died – an old man I loved very much. I used to sit on his knee at the end of the house and he used to tell me about *Tir nan Og*, all those lovely tales. And he died and my father took me so that I would touch his forehead and feel the touch of death so that I would never be afraid of death again.

I was amazed when I met someone recently – a city person – who just couldn't face death because they had never touched or had hardly seen a dead person. They were going into their forties and they just couldn't take death. Whereas things like death and suffering weren't hidden from us. They didn't hide people who were in pain and suffering. One went to sit with them and visit them and listen to them moaning and groaning. And one knew death from a very early age. You knew what was best in life and you knew what one had to put up with. I remember longing for that old man because he was such a lovely old man and I thought my heart would break when he died and I realised he wasn't going to come back.

So in that way, one's faith was strengthened by one's parents. Through experience. And through experience of being sent with food, quietly, to those who had nothing. From my earliest days this would happen. I would be sent off with milk to someone who had lost their cow or who had young children.

This would be happening every day in life. I don't remember ever a day when we weren't doing this kind of practical work of charity or sitting up with people who were dying or dead. You lived your faith right from the word go.

Your faith was all you had. You had nothing except your faith in God. You had no bank-book. No money. I got my first pair of shoes when I went to Blairs – you wore the hand-me-down tackety boots of your brother from November to March. But everybody was poor. Everybody had nothing. Nobody had any money or new clothes. So nobody was rich but nobody was poor either. The vision or the thought of poverty never entered my mind until much later in life. I didn't realise that people felt poor, because we didn't feel poor although we had nothing.

The great Celtic thing too is that you mustn't lose your dignity. You must remember that you have great dignity as a created being and never lose that dignity. And that's why our blessing was never to have experienced the industrial revolution or the post-industrial revolution period in the Hebrides. We never lost our dignity. Nobody ever snapped his fingers and said, "Do this," or, "Do that." You had nothing but you got up in the morning monarch of all you surveyed. That was it.

So one got one's faith through experience early on in life. By the time I went to college, I had experienced everything – pain, suffering, loss, death, and the joys of living, and a great zest for life.

The Hebrideans have a great zest for living. You love the good things of life; I mean, not good by city standards, but you love, say, a pot of good dry potatoes with a piece of butter, things like that. The good things of life. And the freedom of wandering out. I can walk out for ten miles and nobody is going to say, "What is he after? Where is he going?" You're free to go and do your own thing and be yourself. That is the joy and the dignity of being a Hebridean and a Celt.

Our outlook in life is so entirely different to anyone whose outlook is a by-product of the industrial revolution. You take a Uist man who would have gone to work in the gasworks or somewhere three generations ago. His grandchildren will be getting up in the morning and worrying about the rent, and worrying about the job, worrying about what their boss thinks about them, and worrying about promotions, and so on. Whereas the grandchildren of the brother who stayed in Uist will be laid back about life. You see, it was a desperate tragedy, the industrial revolution. Mentally, it stripped people bare of dignity; they weren't their own people any more.

But those who stayed behind kept that marvellous dignity. They might not have much to show for it and their backsides might be showing through their trousers, but what does it matter? None of that matters. I don't have to buy suits of clothes now that I'm in Uist because nobody cares. I don't have to dress up. That's my privilege. We don't have to keep up with the Joneses. We are the Joneses.

Tex Geddes

Soay (Skye)

Several Hebridean islands bear the name "Soay", derived from a Norse word meaning "sheep island". Most are so tiny that they are useful only for grazing and appear on maps, if at all, as anonymous specks. But the one to the west of Elgol on Skye is larger than usual at three miles by two, and has attracted a fair amount of attention in the past. It supports a small population – thanks to the determination of Peterhead-born Tex Geddes.

Tex – the nickname stuck after it was earned during wartime exploits with a Red Indian colleague – first went there with author and naturalist Gavin Maxwell. The two met in the army and, having spotted the abundance of sharks off the west coast of Scotland, decided that their post-war future lay in hunting "these bloody great fish" for their liver oil.

The business thrived and Maxwell acquired Soay to establish a small processing factory. Tex decided to go it alone, and when the island had to be sold at the end of the 1940s because of the decline in demand for shark oil, he bought it.

We talked in Elgol where he was unloading prawns. It was early July, but the late afternoon was cool and drizzly. Straggling tourists paused to drink a cup of coffee from a nearby kiosk, and turned to head eastwards, towards Broadford. Soay, three miles away, formed a grey backdrop to our conversation.

When I went to live there, I discovered that I couldn't turn a sod on it. The people were all crofters and fishermen and I found out that I couldn't be a crofter and a landlord too. It was impossible.

So I gave the island to my wife. She was my landlord and I was a crofter.

Well, through the years – going back to last century – the people of Soay had been forever wanting to be evacuated, and they started on about this again. It came to a head because the steamer used to call twice a week, and they wanted it to come three times a week. So someone figured that it would be cheaper to get rid of them from the island altogether than to give them three steamers a week. They said, "Right then, we'll evacuate you," and in 1953 the whole lot – about 30 people – went to Mull.

They tried to get me to go too. But they couldn't. That's where I buggered up the Secretary of State. You see, they couldn't call it an evacuation because I was a crofter and I was still there with my wife and my little boy of three.

The powers that be did everything they could to get me off that island. They told me there would be no communication with the outside world – no telephone, no steamer service, nothing. So I told them a wee story about Maclean of Duart and Macneil of Barra. They were arguing over which of the two was the oldest clan and Barra said he had an ancestor in the ark, and Maclean said, "Did you ever hear of a Maclean that didn't have a boat of his own?" Well, I was like Maclean. I had a boat of my own.

So the Secretary of State said, "You'll die over there. There's nothing for you to eat. The soil is not very good." And I told him that I quite agreed but that there was a damn good farm between there and America and I would plough that. Aqua. Water. Sea. So I ploughed it and I'm still there.

The day the bastards took the telephone away from Soay, I was ill – I'm a disabled ex-serviceman. I was coughing blood and I thought my lung was finished. I got across to hospital on their boat and I asked them to leave the telephone for my wife and my little boy. But they wouldn't. They had orders to take it away. So I said, "Right. I'll make you pay."

I began making a fool of the Secretary of State by getting my friends to send me overnight telegrams from London. Or they'd register and insure parcels for a hundred quid – there might have been a brick in them. "Deliver it old boy – either that or give me the money." So eventually they gave up and put in the telephone for these telegrams.

After a while, I wrote to the Director of Education and asked if he was going to have me put in jail because I wasn't going to send my son – who was then five – away to school. There was a school on the island, although they'd taken away all the desks, but I was told they couldn't find a teacher for it. So I said that if they couldn't afford to advertise, I would. So I did, and I got about 20 replies. One boy with a teacher for himself. Didn't I make them pay?

Soay now has a population of 13 – more when one of the houses is in use by its owners as a holiday home. Tex's son, also a fisherman, returned to the island after leaving agricultural college and lives there with his wife and two children. Another family and a handful of individuals complete the community. Others have come and gone over the years.

People talk about getting away from it all, of living off the land. It's a lovely place and they call it "paradise". Oh, we've had them by the square bloody yard on Soay. But they don't last. They come wanting to live the life and they're not equipped for it. I remember once, I needed a boat and I had to make it. First of all I had to make a chisel, and I needed a great big nail and I had to make that too. These comic singers come here and they don't know how to grow tatties or clip a sheep.

See all those damn tourists going by? Dozens of them come to me and say, "You live over there? We'd love to go over for a trip." I'd take their balls off if I got them over there on trips. If you dropped a £5 note on the path on Soay, it would lie there for a week or somebody would pick it up and give it back to you. There's no lock on my door. Never was.

I'm not anti-social, but the last bloody thing I want is trips. Sometimes yachtsmen put in, which is a nuisance. Quite a number have read about me in Gavin's book, *Harpoon at a Venture*. If I'm busy, if I'm cutting hay, I'm not on holiday the way they are. If they think they're going to get me to stop and sit all day blethering and wasting my time, like you are, they can all go to hell. And I very smartly tell them so. I just say, "Piss off and go and have your holiday. I haven't got time to be talking here with you."

You know this bed and breakfast thing? I think it's the most degrading bloody profession there ever was. That's my own personal opinion. If you're hungry, lassie, I'll give you a bite to eat. If you're cold and wet, I'll give you a bed. But I'm damned if anybody is going to get my bed while I sleep in the barn. There is no nonsense like that on Soay. We don't need that.

A tall, spare figure, Tex Geddes alternated in a gentle voice between edginess and humour. I irritated him when, with Hebridean winters in mind, I asked whether his was a hard life. The climate, he promptly assured me, is better than Skye's and even if it is bad, he can have the best in home comforts: "All you need is a few dollars and there are plenty of them in the sea if you've got the guts to go and get them."

His assistant is Biddy, an attractive young woman who lives with him and his (ex-Cheltenham Ladies' College) wife.

I put a funny little advertisement in the Country Gentlemen's Association magazine asking if there was a student or a school leaver who would like to come fishing in the summertime to a small island where there are no shops and no roads. A man rang me up and said, "I have a daughter..." And I said, "A daughter? I don't want a daughter." He was an army major who had been in Benbecula with the rocket range and eventually he persuaded me to give her a try. So she came, and so did three young men. I took the girl. I could teach her. She has been with us for eight years.

People ask, "What do you do over there on Soay?" Christ, I'd give them all a job. I am very busy. There are lots of things to do. I've got a couple of hundred sheep, ten or 20 cows, and Highland ponies. Last night, for instance, Biddy and I clipped a sheep at 11 o'clock. We had a gathering and we'd missed three and on our way home we looked in a shelter and we saw one. So we went home, had our supper, and went back and clipped the thing. Then up this morning and away to sea. Tonight when we get home, we have the ponies to look after. Things like that.

Then they say that there can't be any social life there. What does that mean: "social life"? Does it mean going to a hotel for a drink? Or a dance? We'll all bloody soon have a dance. Or if we want a drink, we just take the cork off the bottle. It's quite simple.

Martin Lunghi

Uig, Coll

In 1985, Martin Lunghi and his wife, Elda, gave up a comfortable middle class life in Edinburgh in exchange for two acres of ground on Coll and a cottage which had no sanitation and little running water. Elda has now returned to full-time studying and Martin does wood-carving and hopes to have his writing published. Money is very tight.

Born in 1940, he had been an academic before moving to the island; his wife – 13 years his junior – a home economist. As she was away at college, he was at home alone when we met.

I'm originally from the South London area. Like a lot of people, my parents moved out from the suburbs to a more rural district as they became slightly more affluent. We ended up in a nice little town in Surrey. It was very charming and I still think of it very much as home and I still have a nice warm feeling when I approach that area again. Up here, much as I might like the setting, the scenery, the people, enjoy what I'm doing, it's never for me had that feeling of home. I always feel slightly alien here; which is a curious feeling. I get this lump of nostalgia when I hear a South London accent or a Surrey accent.

After school, I studied engineering for a bit and soon became disillusioned with that because it wasn't quite what I thought it would be. I was of the generation brought up with *Children's Hour* – Larry the Lamb and Dennis the Dachshund – and there was a character called Mr Inventor. Mr Inventor was my childhood hero when I was about five. I wanted to be an inventor and make things, so I ended up going into engineering. But engineering then didn't have a great deal to do with making things and I got disillusioned.

But I did a sort of subsidiary course in psychology and I grew interested in that and went on to do that academically through a number of universities all over the country – and as a profession for quite a number of years as well.

I worked in Sussex in the Swinging Sixties – absolutely a heavenly time and a heavenly place to be. There was an extraordinary impact of music and colour and setting. Very vivid. It had a tremendous effect on everyone. It was a very romantic era – an era of relaxing of constraints of all sorts. You felt as though psychological barriers had been lowered or removed so that you could think in all sorts of fresh ways and do all sorts of things that hadn't been possible, or had been thought very difficult, before. It was possible to think the unthinkable, to do the undoable.

And I think that when you go through a period like that, you don't understand or appreciate the impact until later. So, retrospectively you are influenced. And possibly being here in a rural setting is a reflection of something of the ideology of the Sixties. Notions about a rustic idyll, about what a better way of life is, about man's nature being tainted or distorted by the artificiality of urban settings – nice little clichés like that – bite deep and have meaning for you at a certain age. You think, "I do seem to be living a life which is full of clutter, full of things I don't really believe in, doing things I never really chose to do, going in directions I didn't really choose to aim for, buying things I don't really want."

You don't sit down and think all this. It's part of the *Zeitgeist* of the era you are brought up in, and it permeates your nature.

I came to Scotland first of all as an academic. To Edinburgh. And Edinburgh was a beautiful place. I didn't know where it was before I went there. I was only vaguely aware of where Scotland was.

[Laughter]. It was somewhere north. I had this image of it being full of engineers with curly hair and freckles.

But essentially, Edinburgh was much like any other city and I began to enjoy the freedom of the countryside. It's quite dramatic – the sea and the hills and the mountains. The wildlife, the castles, the physical geography of the place was exciting. To me, the job was interesting, but it was sort of incidental. The people I could take or leave; people are people anywhere really, although there are one or two special people we have retained contact with. But places seem to have a specialness and, coming from the south, Scotland seemed very special. Before that, I had toured the major cities on the Continent and certainly I felt a lot of impact from what I'd seen and what I'd done. But after I came to Scotland, I never went away any more. I didn't feel the need to go off and tour any more. That might have been incidental – you do get sick of touring – but, as I say, geographically Scotland was special.

The wildlife was super. I was never interested in birds before, but the excitement of seeing my first colony of guillemots was incredible. I couldn't believe it. It was down by St. Abbs Head. Suddenly I rounded a headland of rock and there they were. The smell, and the noise, and the jostling. All those tiny little "penguins" sitting there. And the Bass Rock: the colony of gannets was just overwhelming.

I built a boat so I could get much closer to all this stuff that turned me on so much. I could get right under this colony of gannets on the Bass Rock. They were all over me, swirling over my head, defecating on me from a great height. [Laughter]. It was so exciting. Sometimes I felt it was bringing you nearer to God. I don't believe in God at all, I'm completely non-religious, but that was the sort of sense I had.

So you can see the sort of steps I'm taking. Once you get to that point where you're working at one thing in the city, and you're finding yourself delighted and awed by other kinds of things, increasingly you find yourself thinking, "Why am I doing so much of one thing and not so much of the other? Why am I doing so much of what is humdrum and not doing what is more spiritual for me?"

Of course, everyone feels like that. I worked with an exceptional group of people in one of the colleges in Edinburgh. It was in a psychology department with sociologists and psychologists and we all thought very much in the same way. This same sort of feeling lurked in the soul of each of them, I think. In their different ways they all understood this notion of wanting to turn away from one thing towards another. And, interestingly, when I did eventually break away from the academic world, from the city, this seemed unsettling for those who remained because a barrier had been removed. Perhaps they saw that what had been a dream that you talk about at coffee time, a fantasy, was a reality. It was something that you could do. You *can* take that step. So they had to look more seriously at what they were doing themselves. There was this feeling of restlessness created by one of us changing.

It's always the same. I have noticed that when I have been one of a group and someone has left for whatever reason, you think, "Gosh. They're going to do wild, exciting things and I'm stuck here. Boring old me. I want to do something with my life as well. I want to take control and be wild and imaginative."

You sense that you've been a pawn a lot of your life. You sense that in childhood, at school, and university, you've been passively following prescribed lines of thinking and behaviour. You're achieving goals and ends which have been defined for you. You have your house and telly and your digital watch with a snooze alarm. These are goals which are defined for you and you aim for them in prescribed ways. And it's breaking away from that mould which is the difficult thing.

So a sort of choice is cropping up. There is a feeling that a lot of the time you're living where you can in order to do your work. The alternative is simply to work at whatever you can in order to live where you want.

Once you start thinking this way, you start looking at places which are available, places where you could go and live this fanciful life-style. So you begin looking at adverts in estate agents' windows and you see idyllic little cottages for sale in idyllic little places surrounded by panoramas and beauty and inaccessibility.

We got onto a very good thing actually. You get the details from the estate agent, you agree to go and view the property, you get the key, you go off, and the places are usually empty – a derelict church, places like that – and you can spend the weekend living there. So, really, you get a free weekend's lodging. And we did this for a couple of years. It was a wonderful way of life because it's totally future-orientated. It's the stuff of dreams. You never actually have to commit yourself.

I started to do this before I got married and when I got married I carried on doing it. And I suppose as you go down that road you start getting more serious and persuading yourself that you ought to put in a bid every now and again.

There were some very beautiful places – really incredible settings – which, in retrospect, I think I would have been happier in than this. My wife's first impressions of Coll were stronger than mine. I'd never actually thought of an island. There was a place on Eriskay but I never went to see it because I couldn't get there – it would have taken days.

We came here on a weekend to look at the place and it was OK. It was fine. We went down to the beaches at Hogh. And the land seemed good – we had this idea of using the land a fair bit. The general impression was quite positive and my wife said, "This is wonderful. This is it." And I think her enthusiasm carried us through to putting in a bid.

This was the first place where we put in an offer and it was accepted. So, in a sense, it was pure chance that we came to Coll.

We recognised it from the beginning as an experiment which might go wrong. We didn't see it as somewhere where we were going to end up for ever. It was in the spirit of, "This looks fun. Let's have a go at this," that we did it.

And so we came over. That was the end of our mainland phase and the beginning of our island phase. We started our life out here doing a number of things: trying to cultivate the land, bringing up children, improving the house, and doing some sort of work.

At first, Martin stayed on in Edinburgh to support the family while his wife, their baby son, and Elda's two daughters from a previous marriage – both of whom have now grown up and left home – moved to Coll. The separation was difficult. Usually the couple were together only for one weekend in every two or three weeks. When the opportunity to take a small redundancy payment arose, they knew the time had come to sever their link with urban life.

Elda found work variously as a home-help, a seamstress, and a school secretary. Martin did some labouring and carpentry. There were hens for eggs, and goats for butter, cream and ice-cream.

Does he miss the security of a monthly salary?

Not really. No. I quite like the uncertainty. In fact, in my last job the certainty sort of frightened me sometimes and I disliked myself for being so comfortably cosseted by it. It was the only job I ever had which had security of tenure. I could have stayed there till I died, and it was like looking down this long tunnel with a coffin at the end.

I'm very, very poor. But part of the excitement, for me, of living this life-style is not knowing where my next meal is going to come from. But I've got a hell of a lot of potatoes out there. [Laughter]. So that keeps me going for a long time. You can live off very little in terms of food.

Of course, the rustic idyll is always a fantasy. For example, you can't escape consumerism. Consumerism is so much part of my character that I bring it with me.

I do miss access to things that are important to me – things like bookshops. When I go back to the mainland, I really have a feast of bookshops and tool shops – things like that. And I miss being able to travel. Remember, as a mainlander a lot of my life was spent, at weekends, getting in the car with the family and going off to wild, new places. Of course, you can't do that here. In an odd way I miss that. In a sense you are always at the destination you used to be heading for. But apart from these things, I don't really miss a great deal. I still find great joy from the open spaces, whether it's from the sea or the hills, or the heather changing colour. Although, these things are not peculiar to Coll – I get the same feeling in Caithness. I found great joy on Arthur's Seat in Edinburgh. I think I would get the same kind of buzz from any beautiful, vast, open space.

My wife always had a tremendous natural gift for growing things and enjoyed our outdoor life but she also has a strong spiritual and intellectual side to her. She became an active member of a local band – she plays the whistle and the fiddle – followed a course in lay-preaching, and, through working in the local school, developed a strong interest in teaching and education. She gets on very well with children. She's got this great, open, joyful nature which invites children – but at the same time she's no pushover; she can control them and be fierce. So she'll be a super teacher.

She still likes the island very much but she just needed a better standard of living and she couldn't see how it was going to arise here. Now, what will happen at the end, we don't know. That's another uncertainty.

She's got our little boy with her. She said she would worry about him being here and it turns out that he is getting such a kick out of being in a big school rather than a wee school. He has lots of friends to play with there.

Obviously she doesn't know where she is going to be teaching. We'll see what happens. We might try living in two places – we managed living apart for a while before – or I might up sticks and move to wherever she is. We'll see what happens.

Mary Morrison

Penmore, Mull

Originally from Skye, Mary Morrison has lived in Mull since she went to teach there in 1935. She has been both the daughter and the wife of a crofter.

I think crofting is the natural way of life that keeps communities together in the islands. If you didn't have land work, what would you put in its place? The people wouldn't be there. Crofting people would disappear. And there is a natural progression in the life of crofting communities – especially since they got security of tenure from father to son – which makes for rooted families.

I think rooted families are very important. There are an awful lot of people up and down the world now who have no roots. If people know where their roots are, it gives them a pride. Genetically they know who they are, if nothing else. And apart from that, there were always certain qualities that went with families. They go right back to the clan system. Qualities of tenacity, and hospitality, and kindness, and sociability.

My people were evicted from one part of Skye to another. That was four generations back. They were evicted from Boreraig in Skye to Skulamus – that's where my people were, where I was brought up.

My father was a small boy when his family were evicted. That goes back to 1853. He remembered the evictions, the people being put out of their houses. He didn't talk about it a lot, but he remembered it.

I think that hearing about it coloured my attitude to things all my life. I think it probably does colour one's politics somewhat – although it's not fair that it should because you can't just judge things now by what happened a hundred years ago. Can you? But I think it may colour my thinking without me being aware of it. Just like any experience does.

I can remember that it impressed me at the time: the idea that my people had to go off like that with nowhere to go. And it probably also made my idea of family life and home life very important because it's a natural thing that if you lose something it becomes more valuable in your ideas than if you're surrounded by it and you've no problem about having it.

Quite a number of my family went abroad. I've got relations in Canada and, I'm sorry to say, in South Africa, and in Australia.

I've visited the Canadian ones but I wouldn't visit the South African ones because I don't approve of the way people make their money there. But they had to go somewhere I suppose. Everything is relative, isn't it.

An Act of Parliament in 1886 granted crofters security of tenure. Ninety years later, a further Act empowered them to purchase their ground. Mary Morrison is unsure whether this right to buy is a good thing.

It depends on the crofter. The crofter who knows what he's about and has respect for his land, I think, should own it. But of course, there's always the crofter who turns it into cash and sells it to the next guy who comes from the south. I don't approve of that. Having crofting in my blood, I believe that a croft should be used in some sort of way peculiar to the land. Even if you don't turn it with a plough or scatter seed on it, I think you should use it for something to do with agriculture – like cattle, or sheep, or even growing trees in a reasonable way for the environment.

If you're connected with the land, you're very close to nature. It gives you an understanding of what is around you, an understanding of the processes of nature and all the different creatures in it, and also, an understanding of your fellow man.

Supposing you had your neighbour in the next croft. You would be aware of his problems and you would be ready to help him out with them. Or, if he had difficulties in surviving, you would help him out if you could. You would have loyalty to people like yourself who were dependent on the land.

Your fellow man is part of nature. Isn't he? It's rather a radical idea this, but, generally people put themselves on a different plain from all the other creatures that are on this planet. Why should they? Who says that they are different? Who said that in the first place?

Maybe they think a bit more, but that's only because their brains have evolved a bit more from the ape.

But is this empathy with nature still intact as we head for the end of the 20th century?

I think so. Both in the people who are indigenous to the island and in a lot of the people who have come in. They have developed this. I think living on the island is bound to change people. Perhaps, for some, the very fact that they came here in the first place meant that they were ready for some kind of change in their attitude to life.

It's impossible to generalise on how incomers fit in. Some of them fit in very well indeed. Some of them don't fit in at all. The people who come in for a job of work naturally fit in better than people who just come because they like it and want to settle here. Their culture is different and they're not inclined to have much interest in our culture at all. They more or less bring their own culture with them. But the young who have come here to work and have brought up families here: they fit in perfectly well.

There are the remains, if you like to call it that, of the Celtic culture here... Maybe that's a bit pessimistic. Maybe it's beginning to get better again now, but it did go down very much in the last 30, 40 years. For example, there is very little Gaelic spoken now at all in Mull.

I think the future of Gaelic really rests, probably more than anything else, on the young children in the [Gaelic-medium] playgroups. I think if there is a future for Gaelic, that is where it is. The playgroups will be on-going. These young children will be growing up, and if their education is continued in Gaelic in the ordinary schools, and if the will is there to talk it in the homes, then it will survive. Failing that, no amount of money is going to keep a culture alive. I don't think so.

I think very often when a culture is just on the edge of disappearing people begin to try and pull it back. It's a well-known thing in all ethnic groups that this happens.

Gaelic was my way of life. I had no English when I went to school. I didn't have a word of English and I think I and many others like me would damn the sort of idea that children who are taught Gaelic are at a disadvantage, or that fluent speakers of Gaelic are at a disadvantage. I think that is the most ridiculous fallacy that was ever put in the minds of people.

Right down through the years, from the earliest suppression of Gaelic, people were made to think that children with Gaelic were at a disadvantage. Luckily, my parents didn't feel that way. Many other parents didn't, but many, many parents did – especially parents who were working on big estates and places like that. They thought it was the proper thing for their children to be able to speak English.

Very important people were always sent back to England to be educated. And then they came back and they insisted, very often, on their workers and their children talking English. It was all part of the social set up then.

There wasn't so much of that on Skye [compared with other islands where crofting is less widespread] because crofting tenants are a pretty tenacious lot. They stand up together. They are united more. But on big estates on Skye and everywhere else, workers and their children had that idea: you must talk English to the gentry.

My way of life was the way of a crofter's child. This is going back 60-odd, 70 years. There were so many other things that went along with the way of life – like croft work and all the things that pertained to it. It was a completely different way of life from, say, the nine to five lifestyle.

It was very hard. You had to do your bit. Of course, I was away from home since I was about 12 because I went away to secondary school. But, even so, in holidays you had to work, do whatever was going on at the time – haymaking or peat cutting or whatever had to be done.

I went to school in Portree. But in those days you never got home at weekends even though you were only 25 miles from the school because there was no public transport. It was a very big wrench. But it was worse when I went to Glasgow. Some people are more homesick than others. I was one of the unfortunate ones who were very homesick. It was devastating. Homesick for people and homesick for places.

I went to Glasgow when I was just turned 17, and it was quite a thought in those days.

There were three of us who were reasonably well educated – you know, beyond secondary school. My older brother had gone to university but he was killed in the First World War. And then my next brother took a degree in Glasgow University, and so did I. There were eight of us and I was the youngest.

It was amazing that poor families could do that in those days. It must have been a tremendous sacrifice. It was taken for granted that if you had the ability, you carried on. You really didn't think of the sacrifice it meant for your parents.

The importance traditionally placed on education was mentioned again and again as I travelled throughout the islands. But it seemed to me that in the young people of the Hebrides today this emphasis was no greater and no less than elsewhere in Scotland. Mary Morrison agrees that things have changed.

The young are now able to take up so many different spheres of life that don't need quite so much, perhaps, in the way of education. There are many more things going for them. In my time there were very limited possibilities: teaching, the ministry, medicine if you could stick it out for such a long time or if you could afford it. And, really, that was about it. Otherwise you went to sea or did something like that and got yourself pulled up.

Anne McGeary

Daliburgh, South Uist

Anne is a 26-year-old nurse. The daughter of a lawyer, she was born in Lanarkshire and spent most of her childhood in Ayrshire. In January 1991, while working as a midwife in Saudi Arabia, she found herself caught up in the Gulf War. She flew home and went to work in the hospital in Daliburgh, South Uist.

We met in October of that year. Anne had resigned and was leaving the island the following week.

I came up for the interview and it was a fantastic, glorious day. I was smitten by the place – by the beaches and the scenery. And the interview was very nice. Very civilised. "This is lovely," I thought. And they gave me a very quick date to start. And it was promotion.

So it was a step forward for me because it was midwifery and general combined. But it's more geriatric than midwifery up here. [Laughter]. So that's the main reason why I'm leaving.

Seemingly, there were a lot of deliveries at one point, but all the girls tend now to go to Glasgow – for first babies anyway because of the risk of Caesarean sections or whatever. Women having their second or third can have their babies here. That doesn't mean to say there aren't any difficulties with them, but it's safer.

But I've done 10 or 11 deliveries since I've been here, which has been nice. Midwifery is cheery – although it can be sad as well. It's very cheery, and it's with young people, and there's chit-chat. And it's independent. You're on a one-to-one basis with the woman and her husband, and it's a very privileged thing to be with somebody when they deliver.

You can always get some right weirdies. [Laughter]. It's not all a bed of roses, don't get me wrong. Some of them you can see far enough. But it is nice. And here, it's lovely to see them antenatally, delivered, and post-natally. And then to meet them out in the street is nice too. This is a lovely wee community for that.

Geriatric nursing is very mundane. It's just the same thing. You feed them, you dress them. You're like a robot. There's no communication, basically. You're on autopilot. They have a geriatric unit here of eight beds. There is general nursing too, and you get all walks of life through that. I shouldn't say this, but there are an awful lot of alcoholics up here. I suppose you know that. We get them a lot in the hospital and I have a lot of sympathy for them, but I'm not here for that reason. It can be a bit galling. They come in to dry out. They go away. Six months later, it's the same faces again. It's sad really but, I don't know... That's the hard bit coming out in me. [Laughter].

Personally, I think it has been lovely to be here during the summer, but I don't think I could face it in the winter. Not with the gales and all the winds they're talking about. I've been here from April until now and the weather has been OK. I've been hillwalking and I've seen a lot of the island and a lot of the islands surrounding it. And I've thoroughly enjoyed it. But the gales last week were horrific. I wouldn't set foot out the door. I was petrified really. But South Uist as a whole is lovely. If you have a husband and family here, it's great. If you did, I don't think you'd want to go anywhere else. The kids can run about, and it's really friendly.

The people are very quiet and reserved, but they'll come half way to meet you as long as you're prepared to meet them. The girls are extremely nice.

The bachelors? [Laughter]. I wouldn't touch them with a barge-pole. They are a dead loss. They get sozzled. Don't think I'm anti-drink. I enjoy going out and having a drink. But they just get blind drunk. And it's a shame, because I'm sure they're very nice.

No. Not impressed. A good Scottish man: you can't even get one on one of these islands... [Laughter]. They're all very, very shy. Amazingly so.

I'm quite sure if you went to a house, the husband would say hello and then go away. They wouldn't sit and talk, the Highland men. Maybe I'm expecting too much, I don't know.

You tend to find things are old-fashioned. It's the same when you go to church. They all get out pew by pew, and there's nothing spontaneous.

There were two young priests here when I first came – very young and outgoing. But since then, the canon has come and he's much more geared towards the Gaelic masses, and it's like the old-fashioned Latin masses. I find it very unappealing. I don't mind the odd Gaelic mass, but it's continual. Part English and then all the rest in Gaelic, and it's very frustrating. I don't know what he's saying, so what's the difference? And the rituals are more old-fashioned. To explain that – don't take offence – I would describe it as being like me going to your church. I've been a few times to Protestant services and I find them staid and formal. What I'm used to is going to church, and it's all very cheery. It's *nice*. But here, it's very orientated to the kirk-like way. I hope you're not offended, but I find it like that.

I never thought I was ambitious until I came here and I don't think I am really – to the extent of wanting to climb the career ladder. But you do want a bit of feedback from your work. I come off shift absolutely shattered and I think, "What have I done?" I don't really feel I've gained anything. Basically, I don't really think I'm using the qualifications I've got.

So I'm going home for two months and then I'm off to Abu Dhabi. It's different from Saudi Arabia. You can drive, and go to the bar, and sunbathe. Two girls are going with me so, fingers crossed, we'll enjoy it. It's off to a bit of fun and a bit of sun.

Philip Newell

Iona Abbey

Canadian Philip Newell and his Scottish wife Ali are community wardens at Iona Abbey – home of the Iona Community, an ecumenical body existing under the auspices of the Church of Scotland. Until the spring of 1988 when they took up their five-year appointment, the couple were living in Canada, where Philip was a university chaplain.

Thirty-seven year old Philip talked to me about how he came to the ministry...

I'd gone to Edinburgh to study theology out of interest. I didn't have any plans on pursuing ordained ministry in the church. So my great calling was that one day Ali came home from the university to say that she'd signed us both up for the Church of Scotland ministry. Much to my surprise.

So I didn't have a tremendous ambition or sense of calling. And I would say that my calling – my awareness and understanding of it – has come in the context of actually doing it, and coming to a certainty that this is where I should be.

We are a transitory community on the island in that the real focus of our ministry is back on the mainland, and so people just spend a limited amount of time here.

Each week we are a community of about 125, 130, or so, in three different groupings. One is the resident group who are here for a year or three years or slightly longer, then there's a group of volunteers who come for about seven weeks at a time, and the guests form the third group. The guests tend to come from

Saturday to Saturday for a week. They participate in the life and work and worship of the Community. So it's not like coming to a hotel where the meals are laid on. They peel potatoes and clean the loos and work in the gardens. Out there now in the church some guests are working with Ali on the preparation of the evening service.

So what we do week after week here is celebrate community, and it keeps changing of course. Every week there is a different mixture.

Believing that significant things are happening to people is very much what keeps me going. I think back to a group that came last year... We looked at the guest list and we saw that there were some profoundly hearing-impaired people coming, that there were some recovering alcoholics coming, and that there were some sacred dancers coming from San Francisco. And we thought, "How on earth is this going to work? That's a ridiculous mixture of people."

We envisaged the sacred dancers being up dancing in the cosmos, and our experience of recovering alcoholics is that you don't often get people closer to the earth in some ways – often they have come to hate themselves and hate their bodies. And those hearing-impaired people, we thought, probably wouldn't be able to appreciate the music of the sacred dancers...

By the end of the week, in fact, what happened was that there was some very simple circle dancing out in the cloisters and it was amazing to be part of that event. The recovering alcoholics were out there dancing, using their bodies, and the deaf people were able to dance – in some cases for the first time in their lives – because they'd been taught by the dancers to follow the rhythm by feeling the vibrations.

And in weeks like that people thrown together have quite a shift in their world view, because no longer are sacred dancers some sort of weird lot from the west coast of America, and no longer are the hearing-impaired seen as people who can be excluded from a dance, from a musical event, and it's not necessary for the alcoholics to carry on with their hatred of themselves.

So things happen here even when we really give up hope!

The community has always had a very strong emphasis on the value of people living together and sharing aspects of their lives. And, of course, that's so much what the abbey is about week in, week out, with guests coming from all over the world and from a whole range of Christian traditions. And so, I was attracted to this emphasis on community in an age that it so individualistic. Also, the community has always had a very strong concern for the poor and concern for inner-city justice and work with the unemployed and work for the creation of a better society.

Another attraction for me was that it has had a strong peace emphasis. I am myself of the pacifist tradition, although there are others within the community who don't take up that particular line. But we've always had a strong anti-nuclear, peace-making emphasis.

Then there is the importance placed on care for the Earth, and the celebration of the holiness of creation. The place of working out that belief tends to be back in the cities, back on the mainland, but the place where it's often celebrated in quite an accentuated way is here on the island. This is a wonderful place to celebrate the beauty and sacredness of creation because of the extraordinary beauty of Iona and the western isles generally.

One of the things that George MacLeod, the founder of the Iona Community, said about Iona is that it's a very thin place. There is a thin separation between spirit and matter here. And, of course, he wasn't just referring to Iona, but to all of creation being an interwovenness of spirit and matter. So the community has been very involved in ecological concerns.

On this island I'm always very aware of those who have gone before us, of this having been the island where Columba's mission was based, and of it having been a place for pilgrimage for centuries since then. And I find that it's something people are yearning for – a connection with the past, and a universe that is filled with spirit; not an empty, materialistic universe with a tremendous gap between heaven and Earth.

Willie MacKinnon

Tobermory, Mull

Willie MacKinnon was born in Tobermory in 1912 and has lived there all his life. He and his wife Margaret have one son.

When I was in school, times were very bad indeed. There was next to nothing in the houses. Not only in my home, but in others as well. I know one lad – he's still alive and I'm not going to mention names or anything – he was in school one day with his sister's shoes. He had no shoes of his own. One or two children died from malnutrition in those days. It was very bad.

The standard of education was good. It must have been, because I retained quite a lot of what I learned – more than the kids coming out of school today. Some of the teachers were very good.

One teacher was very cruel. He was really cruel. He drank a lot and the kids suffered because of his drinking. He would sometimes fall asleep at his desk.

On the day he was coming, we had no teacher in the morning – a Monday morning. The teacher we had went away to Tiree. She was very good to the children. She belonged to Mull. And when she went away, we were waiting for this man, MacCallum, to come. That would have been 1923 – round about then.

As I said, we didn't have a teacher and it was after what we called "the wee play," at 11 o'clock, that he came in. And I was sitting like this [leaning on his elbow] and he came in and flung his cap on the back of the chair and gave me such a winder on the cheek.

"That will teach you to be slovenly," he says. "Don't sit here with your hand holding your head up."

After that we were all terrified of the man. We'd get the strap. You'd go out and he'd get you up here. Your wrists were bleeding with him. The mothers used to go to the minister and the headmaster, it got so bad. There was one man had him by the throat – he was a brother of one of the lads in his class.

They took him away from here eventually. Down to Dunoon. I don't know how he finished up. He could have been a good enough teacher, but he hadn't the right way with him.

The English teacher, he was a really good man. He had the interests of the children at heart. A fine man. Not dressed the way they are today with jeans and God knows what. He was dressed with a hard collar and tie. Miss MacLeod too, the French teacher, she was good.

We learned to read and write Gaelic, which an awful lot of Gaelic speakers couldn't do. My grandmother, my aunts and uncles, and my mother and father, they spoke Gaelic but they couldn't read or write it. It was never taught in school then. It was handed down from father and mother to the next father and mother. That's the way it went.

I only speak Gaelic now if I get someone I can use it with. There are very few here that can speak Gaelic now. And the way they're going about it, they'll never teach people, because these programmes on television are scandalous. They're just terrible.

That programme *De Tha Seo?* [Game show in which teams guess phrases from drawings made by fellow competitors.] I think it's damnable. It really is. They put two or three squiggles on the board. Now, who on earth is ever going to learn Gaelic like that? It's just money thrown away. That's all it is. The squiggles are like the sign they had for *The Saint*. Two or three lines [drawing in the air] – the saint used to leave that sign any place he went.

Then this *Haggis Agus*. [Cookery programme.] Who is going to learn anything from that? Cookery with things that they never knew in the islands – courgettes and paprika and God knows what.

I don't think Gaelic has got any future. I don't think they'll keep it alive the way they're playing.

It's too bad. Too bad right enough, because it's a nice language. It is. There are no words in it that you could use as really venomous words. You can't get as worked up in Gaelic as you can in English. It tones you down.

The way of life in the islands is getting different. It's not the way it was a few years ago because you've got a big influx of English now. Very big influx of English into the islands. They used to look at us with scorn, you know. And there was always the myth of the Hielan' man running around with a ragged kilt, in the heather, swinging a claymore and chasing a haggis. This is what they thought at first. But they realise now that life in the islands is a damn sight better than what they can get in the cities – with the result that a lot of people reckon that it's the Highland clearances in a different way. They are forcing their way of life onto us. You've got to conform more to the English way of life, not the Scottish way of life. They get themselves elected onto different things. They elect themselves into the upper echelons and then what they say goes. A lot of businesses on the island are owned by English people. Before very long there won't be a Mac left in these parts.

When I left school I started in heavy timber work. You know, with horses, clearing heavy timber. It was going to Glasgow for sawmilling. That's what I was at first of all. I was working here and down at Gruline, and transport was so poor that I stayed down at Gruline, except at weekends. I came home at the weekend on a motorbike.

We had a little bothy put up. It was pretty poor. The wood that was utilised in building it was knocked down at this time of year when the trees were full of sap. They were just run through the mill. The bothy was put up, and the sun came blazing out in June and the wood dried up and there were spaces between the planks. It was candles we had in those days and when there was a gale, the wind would blow the candles out at night. A hard life in those days. All for 37/- a week.

We pulled the timber down the hillside and transported it about four miles down to the beach. Little puffers came in and landed on the beach and when the tide was out you pulled the logs alongside and they hauled them aboard. If the tide was in, you put them on rafts and floated them away out to the boat.

I was about three years at that and then, for a short time, I was working over at the re-opening of the Western Isles Hotel. It had been closed for a long, long time. It re-opened in 1933 and I was working there for a while getting the garden and the tennis court ready. That was what we were at. There were a few of us labouring there for the huge sum of 9d. an hour.

It was built for the opulent society. It is a very big building but there are only 29 bedrooms. That's all. Nowadays they would have about 60 bedrooms in a building that size. More.

The working class never went on holidays in those days. Couldn't afford holidays. They could hardly afford food.

After that, I was working for a family who had a huge house in North Berwick and took Linndhu Lodge up the road there for shooting and fishing. I was more or less a companion for the son. He was a bit older than me. I did a little in the garden and I used to go with him fishing and shooting. We used to go sea angling too. He took a great shine to me. I don't know why. He wouldn't go anywhere without me. He wouldn't take anybody else instead.

I used to go on holiday down to North Berwick with them. I was here on my own from October till May. They would go away in October, back to North Berwick, and I looked after the house. I put a fire on now and again. They were very keen on improving the deer herd. They used to send a lot of maize and I would take it out and spread it on a field up at the top there. The deer got so used to it that they waited for you coming up.

I had a great time with that family. A great life. I was with them for five years.

After that, I was a barman in one of the hotels for 42 years.

In that work you see human nature. Raw, and at its best. You've got to be a father confessor at times as well.

I enjoyed a lot of the customers I had. Had them for a long, long time too. A lot of customers stuck with you. You got a good crack with them. Although, it had its anxious moments. Sometimes you didn't know what was going to happen. You would get some idiot who wanted to start a fight. Somebody throws a glass at you... You get a belt on the ear occasionally...

The pubs are the only meeting places there are here. But I don't know if drinking is any worse here than it is anywhere else. In fact, it must be worse on the mainland because at the weekend there are nothing but stabbings all over the shop – round about Glasgow and all these areas. It's drink that's at the root of that. You don't hear of that on the islands. Do you?

They always say the islands are bad for drink. But if they are bad for drink, people are able to hold it a lot better than on the mainland, that's all I can say.

We used to have a lot of shipping coming in here. This was a great stopping place for the Fleetwood trawlers – deep sea trawlers. Big ships with about 20 men on them. Some of them stopped here to get their gear ready. The weather might be too bad between the North of Scotland and the crossing to Iceland so they sorted their gear here at times. Sometimes they were in for stores.

Some of them, when they left Fleetwood, they would have a little store of drink with them and when that was finished they would be feeling bad. They would force the skipper to come in somewhere. They would throw all the potatoes overboard and the cook would come up and say, "We've got no potatoes left, skipper. We'll have to go in somewhere."

Or perhaps they'd throw all the mugs over the side. "No mugs. We can't go to sea without them." So they'd come in here so they'd get a few bottles of beer as well.

I was offered better jobs away from here. We were just talking about that yesterday. I could have had better jobs, probably with prospects. But, no, I didn't want to leave here. I like to see the sea.

I like to see shipping and I like to see the sea.

Life is not as affluent probably as it is for the ones on the mainland. Although, no... I've got my own house and I've got land and I've two or three coppers in the bank, and I've got a car. So it's a wee bit better than for an awful lot of the ones on the mainland.

There are probably occasions when you wish you had more. But you manage to get along and you'll just take the same as anybody else when you go into the wooden waistcoat.

Angus John Macvicar

Borve, Harris

The drive over the hills from the east of Harris to Borve on the south-west coast offered a startling contrast in landscape. In some places in the east, I had felt that I must be in one of the most ancient places on earth. Here, the scene was one of wild, desolate beauty, of rocky moorland where the rocks themselves looked lined with age. The great boulders scattered around seemed to have been rained down in some turbulent time when the world began to heave into life.

The fertile south-west, with its expanses of lush green machair and golden beaches, was tame in comparison. It was here, in his home in Borve, that I talked to Angus John Macvicar. A 38-year-old bachelor, he gave up his career on the mainland to return to the family croft.

Most crofters have to combine agricultural work with other occupations – fishing, forestry, employment with the local council, for example. But with a 30-acre croft, three others which he sublets, and a fourth belonging to his mother which he also uses, Angus John has enough land at his disposal to allow him to earn a livelihood from that alone.

I was born and brought up here. I went to school at Leverburgh. I did my best to fail the 11-Plus so that I wouldn't have to go to school in Tarbert. I managed that and once I had finished three years of secondary school at Leverburgh, I went to Lews Castle College in Stornoway to do an engineering course. Then I got an apprenticeship in Glasgow – the people who owned the firm were from Ness in Lewis, actually – and I was doing day-release and night-school at Reid Kerr College in Paisley. Eventually I came out as a draftsman and after that I went to work at Yarrow Shipbuilders. I was there for three years at Scotstoun in Glasgow.

Then I came home. That was 14 years ago. My parents were getting on and, having been born and brought up on a croft, I was pretty interested in animals. It is sort of in my people's blood – on my mother's side anyway – to be working with animals. I thought I'd give it a try and see what happened, and when I came home the first thing I did was build this house. And I've struggled away ever since.

I was quite keen to come back, although finance-wise it has made quite a difference. I know that some who stayed in the line of work I trained in now run around in big cars and have big houses. If I was working in that same employment now, I'd be earning probably in the region of about £20,000 a year. Well, on a croft here, you're talking about £7,000 or £8,000 a year.

But, at the same time, I suppose they are paying big mortgages. When I built this house, I got a loan from the Department of Agriculture for 40 years which costs me in the region of £160 a year. If I was still working in Yarrow's, I'd probably be paying £300 a month or something. So I suppose it balances out somehow.

I have 14 head of cattle and 400 ewes. I grow very little – well, oats for the cows, right enough, and some hay. It's mostly rough grazing. On a 30-acre croft here, you're lucky if you have maybe four acres that are arable.

You are on the go all the time. In the winter, you're feeding animals. In the summer, there is always something to do. Springtime, it's lambing, calving, what have you. You've got to be on the stance more or less all the time. I find it just impossible to go away for even a week's holiday. I haven't been away from here for more than three nights at a time since I came home.

I can't say that I missed anything about the mainland after I came back. One thing I just didn't fancy was this sitting in an office for 40 hours a week, or maybe 60 hours in some cases. I was hoping at one point that I might get a job where I could do more outside work, but that didn't come about. That was one of the downfalls: being in all the time. I was used to being out and open spaces. I quite liked the work itself, but at the same time there was something at the back of your mind saying that you're better working outside.

And I used to miss the peace and quiet. When I went to live there at first, it was a hostel I stayed in. A Church of Scotland hostel. There wasn't anything denominational about the place, anybody could live there. Previous to that I was staying in a hostel in Stornoway so I was quite used to that sort of life. But I missed the peace and quiet. The hustle and bustle didn't go down too well with me at all.

And I missed looking out at the sea. Here, by looking out of the window, you can tell what kind of day it is by looking at the sea. Supposing you were deaf, you would know if there was a gale blowing.

There was a fellow from Tarbert, Argyll, staying in the hostel. He was a mechanic and at one time he had worked on a fishing boat. He said to me this day – a Sunday it was – that he would have to go somewhere to see fishing boats. I had been away for three or four months without coming home, and I went with him. We reached down to Ayr and stopped the car and looked out to sea for long enough. It was great to see it...

I think one of my main ideas in coming home was to stop the land going out of crofting, or someone else coming in and taking it over – which happens in quite a few cases nowadays. Every year that goes by, there is another croft that goes vacant. The place is just going downhill.

What you usually find is that if there is a croft and a house and the house is empty, the house gets sold off, providing it is not on a feu, along with the croft, as a croft house. And it is usually bought by incomers, often English people. They have to apply to the

Crofters Commission to ask if they can have the croft as well as the house, and 19 times out of 20 they are told that that will be fine. A crofter would probably get preference if he wanted the croft, but in the vast majority of cases there is no objection to an incomer getting it. So the incomer gets it and they don't have any interest in agriculture at all. They just want it for a wee plot of ground. I'm talking about townships where the crofts aren't so big, where you're talking about maybe five to 10 acre crofts.

If it is a decent house the buyers will probably just repair it, or if it is an old croft house built in the 1900s, 1910s, they will smash it down and build a new one. It's quite easy to sell a house in the south for £200,000 and build a kit house here for £80,000. There are one or two villages south of here where over 50% of the people resident are from outwith Harris altogether.

In this village there are six crofts and there are only three people working them – myself and another two. And I'm the only person who uses the common grazing. One of the other chaps has a young family and I can't see them being interested. They are more interested in computers and things like that. And the other chap's children are all grown up and they're not interested. He just keeps a few sheep.

Most young people go away. If they go to university or whatever and they succeed there, they're not interested in crofting. I remember when I was in school, every night from the age of 11 or 12, I came home and was given a cup of tea and a scone or a pancake or something and it was, "Down you go," to work for maybe four hours down at hay or gathering sheep. Nowadays, they won't take their children. I know a chap who has a boy of 13 years of age and he won't take his son – ever – to a fank. He doesn't want him to get interested in sheep at all.

You don't blame people for not being interested in crofting. You can't *live* on a croft, not on one croft. You have to have a number to make a sort of living out of it. But even then it's difficult.

Crofting has changed vastly. In the 1960s for example, there used to be quite a few head of cattle here, and now there are hardly any cows left. Every crofter had two or three cows. They would have at least one milking cow. Others would have two or three. That's disappeared. People have moved into sheep now.

I think it's due to the cost of feeding cattle and the climate we've had here in the past number of years. As my father was saying recently, this is the eighth bad autumn we've had – really bad, forcing us to buy in hay from the mainland. That cuts the profit down to next to nil when you consider the work involved.

There has been so much rain. In the last few winters there has been very little snow and frost. Snow is a thing of the past round here. You hardly ever see the ground white. Whether it's got anything to do with this ozone layer falling to bits or whatever, I don't know.

Ena Parkin

Backhill, Berneray

Ena Parkin, nee MacAskill, was born in Berneray in 1943, although her youthful appearance belies the fact that she was a war baby. On leaving school, she trained in catering at Duncraig Castle College in Ross-shire, and began a career in private service and hotel and pub management. She met Andrew, an Englishman, while working in London. He was personnel manager in Claridges. They married, moved to the Scottish Highlands, had two children – Anna and Douglas, now aged 13 and 11 – and went to live in Canada.

Berneray's population is on the increase owing to a growing number of locals returning to settle there. In 1989, the Parkin family joined them.

We spoke in her spacious bungalow, occasionally interrupted by the sight of seals leaping around in the bay in front of us.

When I left college, I decided not to go into hotel work. Too boring. Too monotonous. So I went into private service. It's very individual. I'm an individual person. I cannot be a cog in a wheel. I have to be myself. There's nothing anybody can do about it. My tutor at college was furious. She had great hopes for me as a chef. But I said, "No. I'll do it my own way." Each to his own.

I guess I was lucky. Except for one lady I stayed with for three weeks, I've always had the most wonderful people to work with. I've never given a reference in my life. That's saying a lot. Never would I give a reference unless they gave one back to me. No. It was always by word of mouth or a 'phone call.

So I went first to Pitlochry and then to Edinburgh. Then I came back here because my mother was ill one year, and the following year dad broke his leg and couldn't do the harvest. So I spent two years around the croft. And then I saw an ad. in the *Oban Times* and I took this job with an Orthodox Jewish family in London. It was incredible. Best job I ever had in my life. I loved them. They were great. They were good to me. They called me "Eensie". Everything I wanted, I got.

I wasn't just a housekeeper, I was everything. I was a bodyguard because we were under police protection from terrorists. We used to take the kids different routes to school every day. Good old Ena. Oh yes, those were the days. Mail bombs and things. Arab terrorists. I lived in a totally Jewish community practically. The house was a beautiful, beautiful place – real Tudor. The glass at the front was all bullet-proof. It didn't dawn on me at first why it was so tough.

They taught me to be myself really. If you go into a shop and you get shoddy things given to you, you shouldn't be afraid to go back with them. I learned not to be afraid to go back because I had to do her work for her. I would go into a shop now and complain and demand my money back. I would never have thought of it if I hadn't been with them. I'm sure I wouldn't. Didn't want to make a fuss. But I complain now. In a restaurant. Anywhere. Oh yes. Why shouldn't you?

Even here. I went to complain here one day and I hated doing it because we're all related. Every single house on this island bar one is related to me. They're all family – extended, but they're still blood.

I left this Jewish family after four years – or was it five? They became dependent on me. They wanted me to marry this old uncle. Oh God, an 82-year-old frazzled thing. And I would have been very well off, I tell you.

"No thanks," I said. "There's no lust in that man," I said.

"He probably wouldn't last the week with you," said my boss. "So you're alright!"

Anyway, I left them and I went to work for two young tycoons.

Bankers. I mean, "tycoons" was the word. Incredible. I had to look after the two brothers. The father employed me. And I coped with that for a year. Then I went to run a pub off Bayswater Road in London. They said, "Right. You're on probation." I said, "Right. So are you." That's where I met my husband-to-be.

I've always had confidence. That was instilled in me early. Confidence. My uncle, John Ferguson, had the most influence on my life. Brainy man. He used to say, "Be yourself. Be free and be yourself."

I couldn't tell you in a day about John Ferguson, my uncle. They used to come from Edinburgh University to see him. His mind was incredible. He could open a book of poems, and shut it, and that was it: he could recite it. An old boyfriend of mine died last week and I found a love poem that my uncle John wrote for us. 1959. The summer of 1959. June.

He was a great humanitarian. That's what I am first and foremost. I don't care if I don't like somebody, I will do anything to help them if they're threatened. I'm a champion of the underdog. My uncle John was the same. An individual person. He said the mind and spirit of a person should be free and you should learn something new every day.

He was an absolutely incredible man. Wit. Tongue. If he liked you, he'd slander you as soon as you walked in the door. Lots of people were thrown by him. A very nice person. Kind. He was definitely one in a million. But, tragically, he got this wasting disease and he was confined to a wheelchair. I don't know still what it was. A man who was so athletic too. Tall man. Big. Strong. And he died three years ago.

Ena attributes her independent spirit not just to her uncle's influence, but to the fact that she grew up with three brothers. Like many island children of her generation, she left home at the age of 11 to go to secondary school. Life in a hostel in Tarbert, Harris, did nothing to daunt her rebellious nature...

Can you imagine, in those days, playing truant from Sunday school? It was so strictly Sabbatarian. I took the others out. It was like taking them out on strike. Oh what a hoo-ha there was in Tarbert. We were forced to go to church in the morning, to Sunday school in the afternoon, and forced back to church at night. Can you imagine? Walking in Indian file. Boys and girls. So this Sunday I'd had enough and I said, "Right. I'm not going."

"Oh, Ena..."

"No! I'm not going. That's it. Who wants to come with me to the hills?"

So, of course, a lot of boys came; and some girls, not a lot but some. I got six cross-handers. Belted.

"Are you sorry?", they said.

"No!"

You see, this is where uncle John comes in. He said, "Don't let people bug you with religion. Think for yourself. Maybe you will never find what you want, but at least use your brains. Don't be like a puppet."

Nobody will tell me what to do with my private religion. I was brought up as a Protestant, but I've been to mass with Catholics, I've been to synagogues with Jews. I don't care where I go really. I have a very simple faith. It's probably a mixture of the three. I believe in God and all the rest of it, but I don't think I have to go to church on Sunday to be a good person. If you are physically able, it's far better to do other people good. Practising what you preach is far better than strutting up and down to church. I can't stand that. I don't have to prove myself. It's all very well going to church every Sunday, but if you don't do your fellow human being good, what's the point? I'd probably consider myself to be a fairly reasonable Christian. I swear sometimes and I drink and smoke sometimes, but that's between me and the Almighty. I still love my fellow human being.

Sunday is a day of rest here, for sure. But you can still go if you want to and have a picnic on the beach. We're not strict. Far from it. I've had to work on Sundays all my life. But I do conform in some ways – like by not putting a washing out. Well, for one day in the week... I could have it inside if I wanted. No big deal. But why offend the old folk by hanging it outside – and they would find it offensive. But there are other ways I rock boats. I don't care.

I question everything. What was good 20 years ago doesn't hold now for me. The consensus is that the ones that have come home have rocked boats, and people have resented it here. We have made waves on how things should be done, whether it's to do with education or the environment. I'm very much for the environment. No way will I tolerate garbage everywhere. We started a garbage pick-up. We sponsor the kids. Why not?

We're not seen as such a threat now. I don't think I'm exaggerating. They called us "white settlers" at first. Can you believe it? Our own folk. Who are you to come here telling us what to do?: there was nothing physical or verbal, but you could feel that at meetings in the hall. But I was never one to be daunted by other people's feelings. It doesn't worry me as long as I think I'm in the right and my conscience is clear.

I never had any intention of coming back here to live until I was old and in my rocking chair. I bought this plot of land years ago.

I think Hebrideans love their roots. It doesn't matter where you send us. I think most Scots feel the same. We're Celts. You ask any Celt from Brittany, from the Basque region, from Cornwall, from Ireland. Celts are weird people. Very, very deep, emotional, passionate people. We are passionate. Being a Celt certainly hasn't made me feel superior. Not at all. And certainly it hasn't made me feel inferior. It has given me a bit of an edge. I can't define it. It's there. An edge emotionally. My family are like the Italians. I'd do anything for the family. Even if you fall out with them, family come first. I think that's probably what sent us home here.

I wanted to get married down in England. But Andrew wouldn't let me. He said, "No. We're going to get married in the Hebrides." So we did. In Stornoway – they couldn't cope with the catering here. That was the year of the short corn. '76. Drought. My uncle John used to call it "the year of the short corn." Nothing grew. We had a drought from spring to autumn. But it was beautiful. Beautiful for a honeymoon. Andrew just fell in love with the place.

When we lived on the mainland, we used to come back for long weekends. We'd put the cat and the babies and his guns in the car and that was it. We were away. Nothing stopped us. Even when we were in Canada we still came home every year. When we were over there Andrew was very homesick for Berneray. He was travelling all over the States and Canada. He was flying all the time and it wasn't good for his health. So he came home one night and we sat down as we always did for a powwow at the table and that was it. He decided to resign and I agreed with him. Three months notice and we were here. Without a job or anything. No regrets.

My father had died and my uncle John had died and we thought about my mother on her own and my aunt on her own. Plus, if we had stayed our children would have been over there and we would certainly have come back sometime down the road, so we would have been a split family.

I love it here. It's great. I went out to the potato field yesterday and I saw these rows and rows of potatoes ahead of me to do... Then I saw the sun had come out over Pabbay and I thought, "Goodness, what am I complaining about? It's beautiful out here."

You live with the weather as your master here. I'm not being disrespectful to the Almighty, but you live by the weather here. And if the weather says you can't get out of your house, well you don't get out. You become philosophical. You accept things – though I have a terrible temper and I've lived a cushy number away from here, where the weather doesn't really affect you. But here the weather does affect you – you're not going to risk men's lives by asking them to take the boat out. They know damn well they shouldn't, so you don't question them. If I go fishing with my brother to the Atlantic out there, I don't question him when he says, "Do this. Do that." It's different if I'm in my kitchen and I'm cooking. I say, "*You* do this. *You* do that." Each to his own.

I worked hard a lot of my life. Hard. And still work hard. And I'll die working hard, I hope. Hard work is good for you. I'll do any job if I have to. I don't have to work. But that doesn't make me feel proud. I go and do my winkles out of sheer bloody-mindedness. Why should my poor husband have to pay for everything that I want? So I will go and do my winkles; my aunt and I. People laugh at us on the shore there in our oilskins.

"But you don't have to work Ena."

"I know, but I want to do it and it gives me great satisfaction to earn whatever pounds I get at the end of the week."

I love living here. It's lovely to *belong*. I belonged in other places when I lived in England. I was happy there. But this is like being back in the nest. Everybody is round about you. They are so concerned about your welfare – about me, who is so independent! I was fed up with that at first. I couldn't stand it. Now, I rather like it. It's rather nice with Andrew [who works offshore] being away so much. He'll say to the local bachelors, "Look after Ena, now. Make sure you go and see her at nights." And he means it. Where else would that happen but in Berneray? He's away for three weeks, and he's home for three. I hate him being away. I miss him terribly. We've been together 17 years and I'm as crazy about him as the day I married him. He's my best buddy. A great guy.

Rev. Angus Smith

Cross, Lewis

I knew of Rev. Angus Smith by reputation. This was the man who had protested by lying on the slipway when the first Sunday ferry sailed to Skye. He was the Free Church minister who had once campaigned to make that same island dry. Asked by writer and broadcaster Derek Cooper in Cooper's book, Hebridean Connection: "Supposing I were staying here in the manse with you and it was a Sunday. Would you mind if I went out for a walk?", this Sabbatarian's response had been: "Not at all, Mr Cooper, providing you had a doctor's certificate confirming that it was essential for purposes of your health that you went for a walk."

Since my arrival in Lewis, people had looked at me slightly quizzically if I mentioned my impending appointment with him. Those who did not ask outright were clearly wondering if I was aware of his strong views.

So when I pulled up at his manse, I half expected to see a tall, stern figure with a long Old Testament beard. Perhaps, for good measure, he would be clutching a Bible under his arm. The shortish, blue-cardiganed, smiling man who talked to me across his dining-table was a surprise.

I was born in Glasgow, of Lewis parentage. Both my parents came from North Tolsta and they kept up the Gaelic in the home. We always had worship in Gaelic in the home. I never heard worship in English until I was, I think, 20 or so.

We attended a church in Govan – St. Columba's Free Church – and the sermon in the morning was always in Gaelic. When I was a small boy, I used to hear Gaelic on the streets every day. Things have changed. You don't have so many Lewis folk going to an area like that nowadays. There were shipyards and a lot went there for work. But now that work has dried up and there has been a dispersal to the housing schemes and that broke up the Gaelic community to a great extent.

I was brought up in a home which resembled those in Lewis. It was like living in two worlds in a sense. When you entered your own house you were in Lewis. When you went outside you were in Glasgow. It was very much like oil and water. The two didn't mix all that well.

There wasn't a great deal of church-going in Glasgow. There was among older folks, but you had many who had no interest in the Bible. My father and mother were both Christians. They were always discussing the things of the Lord and I came to think of Christianity from the point of view of people who loved the Lord. They loved the Word of God and liked to worship together. That kind of controlled their lives. It gave a stability and purpose to life that in many homes outside, I just couldn't find.

We always had family worship night and morning, and after worship at night-time, it was the done thing, especially if there were friends in, to discuss faith and hope and various texts and doctrines.

In most places in Scotland people don't talk religion. Those who say they are Christians don't talk about Christ and you come to realise that to a great extent, it's not a true thing in their lives at all. Many go to church and say they are Christians and yet you find nothing else in their lives to show that they are. That is a general statement. Not everyone is like that, but I feel that Christianity has gone down. If I go among company today in Scotland and I begin to talk about the things of the Lord, people just can't discuss them. They're not used to it.

But if I go into any home in Lewis and begin to discuss these things, the people take up the subject. They're used to it. They have been brought up that way – well, the Christians anyway, the ones that follow the Lord. Even in homes where you don't have

Christians, they've heard these things being talked about – they have some understanding of them even if they don't go to church.

If you go to Glasgow now, there is no Sabbath. All the festivals and all the rest of it are held on Sundays. On the Lord's Day here, you know it's the Lord's Day. I'm not saying it's the perfect Sabbath. By no means. But it's a different day. You can see it's different.

The word of God tells you how it should be kept. You're supposed to keep it as a day different from all the others. It is one day in seven that God has given us to lay aside all the non-essential duties and non-essential activities so that we can devote that day to the Lord. You see, we have a soul. We are heading for eternity and this world is a mere nothing compared to what is before us. Our real home is in eternity. God tells us that He has given us this day so that we can forget the things of this world and concentrate on the things of the soul, concentrate on the Lord Jesus as Saviour, concentrate on the marvellous Word that God has given us to lead sinners to Himself and to strengthen them and to guide them and to build them up in faith and holiness.

It's wonderful that you can forget everything else on that day and just concentrate on Him. It's a refreshment for the soul that nothing else can give you and this country is missing out on that today. The Sabbath was made for all men and nobody has any right to take it away from us. We should be allowed to have it because we should prepare for God. It's the fourth commandment. You've got 10 commandments and the fourth of these is the Sabbath Day. And it has the same weight as Thou Shalt Not Kill, Thou Shalt Not Swear, Thou Shalt Not Commit Adultery, Thou Shalt Not Covet. And it was meant for the whole of time.

You've got to eat and drink and sleep. These are necessities and mercies, and the Sabbath commandment allows for them. People go to church and the kids go to Sabbath school. Indoors, we like to read scripture and discuss things, or have our own private worship. When I was bringing up my own family, after evening service we'd all be together and have stories from the Bible – we had that every night, they always wanted stories out of the Bible and maybe quizzes and things, anything just to instruct them.

But merely reading the Bible doesn't make a man a Christian. You're not a Christian until your heart has changed, until you come to know the Lord as your Saviour and trust in Him. And when you do, these things become a delight, not a task. They were a task for me before I came to know the Lord, but they are not a task nowadays. I love the Bible because it has got God's mind and God's heart there. It is like a mirror. You hold it up to people and it shows them things about themselves which, unaided, they don't really see too well – the depths of sin, the depravity of sin.

Some people speak of a time and a place, or even a sermon, when they became aware of their sinfulness and they came to the Lord in their hearts and believed in Him. But others who desire the Lord seem to seek Him. For them, it's like the Gaelic proverb: *Cha'n ann le aon bhuille a leagar a chraobh* – It's not with one blow you fell the tree. They have it as a gradual process. Maybe they say first that they don't know the Lord. Then they might come to a time when they think maybe they are saved, maybe they are not. Then they might reach the stage where they say that they understand it more clearly, that they *do* trust in the Lord, He *is* their Saviour.

But basically the work is the same – the Holy Spirit works in a man's heart. He must be born again. He must be changed.

You have got to have a personal confrontation with the Lord. Most people spend their lives dodging it. They may offer up their prayers night and morning, but it's just a sop for their conscience. This is different. This is coming to meet the Lord and saying to Him that it doesn't matter what is going to happen to you, you must meet Him, you must know Him. We were made to be like that. He made us and we need Him. It's an in-built need.

People seek happiness and they can't find it because they don't know what it is. They think of it in terms of money, property, marriage, children. But even when you get all that, there is this basic unhappiness because you've got to come back to the Lord. That's the basis of all happiness and once you know the Lord, it enriches all your other relationships – your marriage, your relationship with kids and other people. You can't hate people. You come to love their souls. You want their salvation. Everything changes.

I lost my brother when I was about 10 years of age. He was 16 and a half. And I began to wonder where he had gone. To heaven or to hell? Did he know the Lord Jesus as his Saviour? And from that I went on to worry about my own soul. I remember reading through the Bible from end to end, trying to find the Lord Jesus. I couldn't find Him. I remember praying constantly, and I couldn't find Him. I went to church, listening very carefully, and I couldn't find Him. And I didn't know how to find Him. When I was at the end of my tether, I prayed to the Lord Jesus – I was only a boy of about 11 or 12 at that time – saying, "I've tried to find You. I've read the Bible, and prayed, and gone to church. I can't find You. I don't know what to do. I don't know how to believe."

And I remember at that very point saying to myself that I'd never had this exact experience before – coming to Christ, throwing myself at His feet, as it were, and saying that I'm leaving myself in His hands to dispose of as He chooses. And I realised that the Lord wasn't hiding Himself at all, that all the time when I thought I wasn't finding Him, He was directing me slowly, gradually, towards that very point. And then a kind of flame came into my heart. I don't know how to express it any better than that. And I realised that this was salvation. I was leaving everything in His hands. He, from then on, would be my Lord, my Leader, my Guide, my God. I just wanted His will, no longer my own. That was my experience.

But since then I have desired that others might come to the Lord. This is the thing. You come to know that a Christless life is a barren life. I have a happiness now, a basic happiness, that is there all the time, and I pity people who don't have Christ.

I know there are people who are against me, people who regard me as an enemy when I stand up for this or that. But I don't hate anyone. I can't hate anyone. I can oppose people, argue with them, but I don't hate them because they have a precious soul and they all need the Lord Jesus just as much as I do. And if they don't find Him in this world, they are lost.

By nature, men don't like being told that they are going to hell unless they change. A man will tell you that he does his best, that he is a good, upright, moral man. And you have to say to him that his best is not good enough, that his heart has got to change. He has got to believe in Christ.

Lots of people hope they'll get to heaven but they want to ignore God all their lives and get there at the last moment – just believe in Him on their deathbeds, this kind of thing. They want the best of both worlds. But I've seen lots of deathbeds and it doesn't work that way. People who live Christless lives harden more and more against God. Even if they got to heaven, it wouldn't be a heaven to them because they have no fellowship with God's people. They have no love for God's Word, no love for the Lord.

If I found a man on his deathbed and I thought he was Christless, of course I would pray with him. I'd speak to him and point to Christ. The thief on the cross was saved at the 11th hour. It can happen, but personally, I don't think very many people are saved at the end.

We have to be honest about these things. Today, hell preaching has gone to a great extent simply because many preachers choose what to believe. They make up their own Bible by chopping and changing God's word. But we have no right to do that.

If you miss out things like judgement, if you miss out speaking about heaven and hell, you preach a kind of sermon which is really emasculating the Bible. There is no Bible in it at all. But in Lewis we believe in preaching the Gospel. That is not just in our church – the Free Church – but in the Church of Scotland too.

The Church of Scotland here is different from that on the mainland. On the mainland – although I'm not saying they don't have some good congregations – on the whole they are as dead as a dodo in spiritual terms. They are mere social clubs. But on this island, I must say, the ministers I meet seem to be men of God who preach the Gospel. There is also the Free Presbyterian Church and its ministers are the same – men of God.

Up to about two years ago, I had no members in my church who couldn't speak Gaelic. Then some people came into the area who had no Gaelic so I had to make provision for them by having an English service in the morning before my Gaelic one, and I find that a few English folk and Lowland Scots are coming to that service. The incomers are not all anti-Gospel, you know. I think some of them come here because they want a Gospel area. Some of them. They want a Gospel fellowship and we have that.

Gaelic speakers like to worship in their own language. And an English speaker, of course, likes to worship in his own language. It's natural. It means more if you worship in your native tongue.

English is a far more technical language than Gaelic. Gaelic very often borrows technical terms from English because engineering and technical schools and industry grew up in the English-speaking world. Gaelic has its own culture. How will I put it? It's bardic. It's poetic. Gaelic songs are full of love and feeling and passion and emotion. Take the word "dear" or "darling" – that kind of emotive term. Seemingly, Gaelic has about 70 words for that, although I don't know them all. So you see how precious it is to have Gaelic.

I was brought up in bi-lingual fashion. I know both worlds equally well. But I prefer a Gaelic sermon myself. And I much prefer Gaelic singing. Much. I find the English singing more artificial. You see, when you sing in English, you learn the tune exactly as it is. In Gaelic you use so many grace notes and everybody can be slightly different but it all merges together into a kind of shimmer. And, to me, it's like the sound of the sea, or the sound of the wind, or all the sounds of nature merging into one.

Mairead Maclean

Coll, Lewis

Twelve-year-old Mairead had returned from the 1990 Mod, in Govan, only a few days before we met. We talked in her home in the village of Coll, where she lives with her mother Lynn, her father Donnie – director of An Comunn Gaidhealach – and two younger brothers.

A pupil at Back Secondary School, she was, like first-years everywhere, still grappling with the complexities of the timetable.

What subjects do you have now that you didn't have in primary school?

Science, French, the library, and I get more technical and much more Gaelic now. My favourite is science and, I think, maths.

How often do you have Gaelic?

Every day. We didn't get much in primary at all, just the basics like saying yes, and about dogs and cats and sheep. Now, we're introducing people, finding out each other's ages and saying hello.

Do you like Gaelic?

Yes.

If you could speak it fluently, when would you use it?

I'm not too sure because English seems to be everything now. I can understand Gaelic but I can't actually write it down because you look something up in a dictionary but then, when you put it down in a sentence, you have to jumble the words up. It's very confusing.

What do you think will happen to Gaelic in the future?

I think it should carry on because most of the schools have

Gaelic classes.

What do your friends think about it?

My friend is from London. She was in P6 when she came here and I think she finds it a bit boring. It sometimes can be pretty boring, but at other times it's fine. When I'm waiting to go into my Gaelic class after the interval, I can't be bothered. But when I get in there, it's fine.

What did you do at the Mod?

I was singing a traditional, a prescribed, and I was in a choir.

What did you sing in the choir?

We sang two harmonies and two unisons. That was *Duthaich nan Craobh* and *Lag nan Cruachan*, and *Hiri mo Chuilean* and *Saoil a Mhor am Pos Thu*? A port-a beul, which was *Suid a' Bhalacha*; and the reel was *Eadar a' Ghearradh*. I like the harmonies best because they have a nice sound to them.

How did the choir get on?

Not too well.

What was the result?

We were against one choir – the Sir E. Scott – and we were second. It was so embarrassing.

What solos did you do?

One was *An Rionnach Beag 'sa Rionnach Mor* and then my traditional – which was my choice – was *Cadal Cha Dean Mi*.

Why did you choose that one?

I don't know, but the other one was so babyish. Very boring. It was about two fish and it was written by Donnie Dotaman. Something for a two-year-old.

Where did you stay in Glasgow?

Our choir was in the Pond Hotel. It was lovely. It had a swimming pool and a jacuzzi and weights. It was really nice.

What did you think of Glasgow?

It's a lot different from here. There are hardly any fields, apart from on the outskirts. And they need a lot of the houses doing up. There are a lot of punks there. I don't think it's nicer than here. I mean, there is no freedom there. It's just pavements and roads. But I liked the shopping and the Mod.

Have you been to a lot of places on the mainland?

I've been down to London and Chester, and I've been to Aberdeen, Glasgow, Inverness, Edinburgh, Inverbervie and Stonehaven. That's just about it, I think.

London was awful. I didn't like it at all. It was covered in graffiti and it was all dusty. It was just awful. Chester was much quieter. It was nice. It had a lot of old stuff – the wall and other Roman things. Aberdeen? I suppose it's a bit cleaner than Glasgow but there are a lot of streets. The shops are good. Inverness is about the same. Stonehaven is just a little town. It had a nice harbour and we went fishing. Inverbervie was a teeny little thing, a bit like here. It had a beach and we were sleeping in a caravan beside a sports centre, so it wasn't bad.

Do you like living here?

It's lovely. I like it because you've got plenty of fields and beaches and freedom. It's got a lot of places you can ride. Even when you're riding on the roads, it's not as bad as it would be on London roads. That's my horse, Sin Agad I, out there. It was on TV, on a Gaelic programme called *Sin Agad E* – we changed its name to that for a day but its actual name is Sin Agad I because it's a mare.

It gets a little bit boring here on a Sunday because you can't do much. If you got caught riding a bike on a Sunday, everybody would be talking about you for weeks. Sometimes my friend stops over here or I stop over at her house. So we're usually indoors doing something or we go for a walk on the beach.

Saturday is very rushed, but it's good. First of all, I squeeze in a ride. Then I go with my mother to dancing for about half past one, all day down to about half past five. Then we do something in town and we come back at about half past six.

Do you go to church on Sunday?

No.

What do you like to do in your spare time besides riding your horse?

Highland dancing, singing, and I'm learning the piano and the chanter.

What kind of music do you like?

Gaelic music mainly. I like Cathie Ann MacPhee, and I like Dire Straits and Status Quo.

What do you watch on television?

The Horse of the Year Shows and the Mod programmes. Sometimes *Home and Away,* if I'm in.

Have you thought about what you would like to do when you leave school?

Yes. Be a vet. But trying to get the grades will be impossible.

Would you mind going away to study for that?

Yes, in a way because I don't want to leave my horse – or here, I suppose.

Do you think you would be homesick?

Well... Not on Sundays.

Jim Corbett

Laggan, Mull

Eventually, the scenery begins to wash over you. You stop noticing the sapphire seas, the white beaches, the beautiful hues of the moorland. But I defy even the weariest island traveller to be unimpressed by the drive down to Laggan on Loch Buie, home of Jim Corbett and his wife Patience. My only regret was that I was there a little too early in the year to enjoy the plethora of rhododendrons in full bloom.

"Carry on past three cottages until you get to the sea. Turn left along a rocky road you couldn't possibly believe anyone lived down. Be brave!", Jim had directed.

This was the ultimate in Scottish pictorial calendar scenery. Highland cattle strolled across my path down onto the sands. Yellow gorse covered the hillside. Behind me, Moy Castle peeked above the tree-tops.

The Corbetts have a family of three: a daughter working in Southampton, a son who was about to join the army, and another son away at school. Tall and cultured, Jim talked to me in the sitting-room in front of a large open fire of crackling logs.

My wife and I moved here from Sussex 12 years ago. But my family has been here since 1922 and the estate now is really a family estate in that my father is in Loch Buie House and he has retained a proportion of the farm which I run for him, and there are three other farms on the estate which belong to my two brothers and myself and I run them as one farm.

There are 21,000 acres; although I also rent a further 4,000 acres which my grandmother sold.

In Edwardian times, and in the early '20s, a lot of West Highland estates changed hands and my great-grandfather bought Loch Buie. He was a brewer. That's his portrait. He was chairman of Watney Combe and Reid in the '20s and '30s, and he had other brewing interests.

So he came up and then my grandmother took over from him for a couple of years, and then my father took it on and he has been here since 1935. He farms in the south as well. He flits back and forward, but I am here permanently.

I did 15 years with Watney's and then came here – having always intended to do so. I was brought up here as a child. I spent a good proportion of my childhood in the south as well, but I spent a lot of time here and I've always felt that this was more home, and that one could make a living here if one put one's mind to it – although running a West Highland estate is not the most profitable way of earning a living.

Between father and myself we run 1,800 ewes and 45 cows. And then there are the deer. We let a bit of stalking. We have the people to stay in the house. We have Swiss, Germans, and British. We'll have anybody if they're nice [laughter], but it has tended to work out that way.

We do it through word of mouth. We started off with one client and we don't let more than a fortnight, three weeks, a year. But it helps a little bit. The first few years we did it, I was the only stalker. I took them out. I still take them out but my cousin comes and helps me now.

What I try and create here is a family house party atmosphere. So they come and stay in the house and they feel as though they are part of the proceedings. They don't feel as though they are paying guests. And they pay one figure and there are no extras. So if they ask for a kipper at 4 o'clock in the morning, they get a kipper at 4 o'clock in the morning and nobody says, "Why should you have it?" Mind you, nobody ever has asked for one.

Do you see what I mean? There is nothing more boring, I think, than going somewhere and everything you do, you're told you've got to pay a little bit more for. So the idea we try and operate here is that everything is included.

And since it's either my cousin or myself or another friend who takes them stalking, we all have dinner round the same table in the evening. And as we've got two parties out stalking during the day, and sometimes three, every stag gets re-stalked round the dinner-table at night. It's great conversation and instead of the stalker going home and the client settling down to a hotel, it carries on the atmosphere – which they like. Well, they keep coming back so they must like it.

I've had one that I wouldn't have back. I've had another that I would probably have preferred not to have had back but he's just booked again for this year and I've accepted.

The one I wouldn't have back was a Brit, strangely enough, and he always wanted something else. It didn't seem to matter what one did for him, he always wanted something else and I think I finally decided enough was enough when he said he wanted to shoot a goat. That was alright. We've got wild goats here and every now and again a client wants to shoot one – they're not uncommon throughout the west. So I agreed.

So he shot one. But, he had a friend staying and he was paying for him, and he said this friend wanted to shoot one too and then he took me quietly aside and said would I make certain that his friend didn't shoot as good a one as he'd shot because he was paying?

Well, I couldn't take that. I said I wasn't having any more goats shot unless the people who shot them ate them – which was slightly a two-edged sword because the goat was duly cooked and I had to eat it with them. Actually, it wasn't as bad as I thought it would be.

We have a cook for the stalking because my wife makes the beds, lights the fires, looks after the house and everything. When they come in cold and soaking wet from stalking, she's there to give them a dram and make certain the fire's on. They have a little sitting-room at their end of the house. Although they use this room too, they like to sit in there and talk – the Germans particularly like to sit and talk themselves and drink beer when they come in. So my wife looks after all that and it would be quite impossible for her to cook the dinner at the same time.

I think running a place like this is a hotchpotch of trying to put everything together. We've got a couple of holiday cottages, the stalking, the farm. We've got a fish farm as tenants.

And yesterday we took delivery of 38,000 oysters. That's another wee diversification. In theory, we're going to have about 150,000 and try and turn over 50,000 a year. It's a three-year cycle.

Three of us are trying it together. A friend of mine who lives just down the road has been running a fish van to Manchester for the last five years – buying shellfish round the island and supplying Chinese restaurants in Manchester. This has been really quite successful and so what we thought was that if we could grow our own oysters, then I'll sell them to him, and he'll sell them to Manchester. So we've got the market already. It's just a question now of growing the oysters. We've done a trial, monitored by the Highlands and Islands Development Board, and it looks quite promising.

I think perhaps the challenge of running an estate is a big part of the attraction. It isn't easy. But it's a wonderful life. It's a good life. You're outdoors most of the time. You've always got something to see for your efforts. There's a tremendous sense of satisfaction – you know, if one can improve the sheep stock, if one can improve the cattle. At the moment, we're re-seeding most of what used to be our hay parks. I don't know whether the weather has changed, but father seemed to manage to make quite a lot of hay in his day, and I seem to be incapable of making it. The weather is always against us somehow. So we now make big bale silage and we're re-seeding all the parks in order to do that more efficiently. It's good to see the parks producing more.

And there's the fact that one has been brought up here as a child. The estate has been in the family for the last 70 years: that is the appeal in many respects. And, it's home.

The only thing I sometimes hanker for – and I'm still involved in it – is the driving. You can see the various pictures of horses around the room; well, I used to drive a four-in-hand. I'm still involved in driving in Britain, although not as much as I was.

I don't think I miss anything else particularly.

The island is quite social in many respects. In the winter, one tends to see all one's island friends. The island entertains itself in the winter, as you might say. There are various sorts of dances, and people tend to have drinks parties and supper parties and dinner parties and things like that. So one tends to see all one's island friends during the winter, and in the summer they tend to entertain friends from the mainland and the south and places, and we tend to do the same. So you've got a sort of summer and winter season, as it were.

Has he ever sensed any resentment from the islanders because of his position as a landowner?

Yes, in the past. I don't think anybody ever came up and said anything to my face. But then, that's not the way things are done. There was an undercurrent of feeling that one could sort of understand and see.

But I like to think that has gone now. I think it existed particularly during the '70s when an awful lot of the older generation passed on and we went through a lean period and it looked as though the community was dying. At one stage we were down to one person in Croggan.

We used to have farming tenants but then, as the years went on, through the late Thirties and the Forties and the Fifties, they gradually died out or retired and in those days it was extremely difficult to re-let farms in this part of the world because the profitability was such that nobody could afford to pay an economical rent and one ended up paying for an awful lot of repairs with nothing coming in. And so what happened was, when my father discovered he couldn't find tenants, he took the farms on himself, bought sheep stock, and started to run the place as one. Our last tenant retired in the mid Sixties and that was at the

Croggan end of the estate. His widow still lives on the place.

But now, although we don't have tenant farmers, we haven't got very many empty houses. The fish farm has filled a lot of houses and we've had various people in from outside to whom we've either let houses or sold sites to build their own houses. I think in years gone by it was a simple matter: anybody that lived on the estate worked on the estate. But today there isn't the work on the estate so it's more difficult to keep communities going.

Croggan now has five families, so that's increased enormously. And I think people outside recognise that. My impression is that it's recognised that one is doing something.

Angus MacLellan

Tigharry, North Uist

Angus MacLellan had been described to me as "the last of the North Uist bards". He was born in 1912, on the croft which is still his home. He spent some time in England employed by the lighthouse service, but returned to the island because of ill health. At the time of this interview a selection of his work was about to be published by the local historical society.

I suppose I started composing when I was going to school. I would compose little verses now and again. They'd be about working on the croft – ploughing and harrowing after a pair of horses, that sort of thing. But I never let anyone know I was composing for a long time. I just did it for my own satisfaction. It was just a pastime. Then, when I started to write some of the poems down, I suppose I took a little more interest.

They would be about the island mostly – some of the things that go on in the township; the way some of the views look at certain times of the year. When you go away, you think the island is the most beautiful place you've ever seen, so some would be about that. That's a kind of homesickness, although I wasn't struck very much by homesickness in my life. You use a lot of your imagination for these things. If you've got the aptitude for putting words together, that's what it comes to. I was hardly ever homesick but I could use my imagination and write something about that. Perhaps the singer or the listener would get much more out of it than I got myself.

Some of my poems were made into songs. I suppose some more

will be when the little book is out, although there are one or two pieces in it which are not suitable for music.

Sometimes it would come quite easily. Other times it would take quite long. It doesn't come whenever you want it. You can't just turn the tap on. You might start composing when you're lying in bed during the night, then you're too lazy to get up to write it down and if you can't remember it, it's gone the next morning. Sometimes I would lose most of my sleep trying to keep mind of what I'd just composed.

But I lost – what would you call it? – the "knack" of writing. I lost the gift, if you like. If it is a gift. If you don't keep up with it, if you let it out of practice, it deserts you. You've got to woo it, the same as you would woo a woman. If you don't keep up to her, she'll leave you eventually.

The island bards composed as the mood took them, I suppose. Some of them, long ago, went round running people down and saying things about them. What would you call it in English? Satire. They were great satirists long ago. But they're not like that now. If they think like that now, they don't let it out. Some of them had crofts, but I think on the whole bards were very lazy. They didn't want to do much work.

People nowadays don't get to hear songs the way they used to because there are hardly any of the old-fashioned meetings like weddings. Now, they go to some distant place and have a big affair when someone gets married. You don't get the songs being sung the way they used to be in the old times when the wedding would be in the house and the dance would be out in the barn. In the past there were many more people in the district and it was on these occasions that the local bard would get his songs sung and they'd get into circulation that way. But nowadays these affairs don't happen.

Up until the late 1920s, the weddings would be held in the house – they were not always in the church. The minister would come to the house.

On, say, the Friday before the banns were declared, there would be what was called a *reiteach*. The groom and a few pals would go to the bride-to-be's house and they'd maybe have a bottle with them to drink and the table would be set and the groom's friends would tell what they were there for. It was just a formality because the people of the house knew what they were there for. They'd come for the daughter of the house. That would be the first part.

Then, on the Sunday, the banns were declared in church, and on the Monday all the womenfolk in the district would go with baskets and parcels of foodstuffs and maybe a cockerel under their arms, and maybe the cockerel would be still gawking and crowing until it got to the house and then it would be killed. Then a lot of women would come in to help pluck the birds. That was the way they collected food.

This would be going on from Monday to Thursday. Thursday was always the day for weddings here. I don't know why. On the day, there would be the ceremony, and the dancing would be going on until the following morning. The couple would go round some of the old folk who perhaps didn't manage for some reason to the ceremony, with a bottle or two. Then, on Sunday, they would go to the church to be kirked. The groom and the bride and the best man and the bridesmaid would go to the church in a very formal manner and take a seat in front of the minister. That was always done.

My father had a shop here and people used to gather in this house. The old bodachs would come for their tobacco and they'd come into the kitchen here and light up their pipes and they'd start yarning away. That was a real ceilidh.

They might talk about the old stories from time immemorial. These go back to the Fèinn in Ireland – the old legends of these warriors long ago. The Fèinn were a mythical band of warriors who used to play their games and keep themselves in good trim for fighting. That was all they did – fighting and playing and hunting.

Or the old men might talk about when they used to go to the militia. That was what later became known as the Territorial Army. They went away there in their younger days and when they came back, it would keep them going the whole winter telling stories about it. They were great story-tellers.

Maybe they would go just as far as Lochmaddy once or twice a year, and that would keep them going in stories. They'd make a story about every little incident that happened. There might be embellishment to a certain extent, but there was no harm in that.

Or the talk might be about the Clearances. They were mostly on the north side of the island, in the Sollas district. People were forced to leave their homes. Some of them were given plots of land on very remote places where there wasn't much for them except a little fishing. The poor people were forced to leave better land and go to places like that. They were cleared away to make way for sheep runs for the proprietor or any of his favourites. In fact, some of them were very nearly burnt out of their homes. Some old women or men who perhaps couldn't walk would be taken and dumped outside, and what little effects they had thrown after them, and a match set to the thatch. Cruel. Absolutely.

When we were young, we didn't really take in as much as we should have about all these things. Later on you were sorry that you didn't listen more, or remember more. A lot of all that was lost.

Jim Johnston

Leverburgh, Harris

Jim Johnston is headteacher in Leverhulme Memorial School in Leverburgh, south Harris. The 57 pupils had gone home for the day and Jim, his wife Marilyn, and baby son Ross, were in the school house when I arrived.

The couple first came to Harris in 1979 to visit Marilyn's sister and her husband. Jim, a Glaswegian, was immediately attracted to the island.

I'd just spent five weeks on the Greek islands and I came up here and fell in love with the place because it reminded me so much of that fantastic holiday. The landscape is very similar. It's windy – the wind is about 15 degrees colder here of course – and there are azure blue seas and beautiful beaches. And when you get to know the people, you just can't help but like them as well.

One of my first experiences of meeting the people was when Marilyn and I came back out of the tourist season and we went for a walk on a very, very cold day. On the way back to the car, we passed a sort of post office, which was the only shop in the whole area and Marilyn said we should get a bar of chocolate. As we walked in the door, the postman, who was behind the counter, was in the process of dissecting a sheep's carcass for his freezer, which really struck me as unusual. We told him what we wanted and he said to give him a couple of minutes to get cleaned up. Then he asked what we were doing there at that time of year and we told him we were on holiday, staying with relations. He asked who that might be and when we told him, he said he knew them well:

"Don't bother with a bar of chocolate, come into the house."

So he took us in and we met this old cailleach who was sitting at the fire and she had very little English so everything we said was translated through the man to her. Then out came this plate of cakes and scones with cups of tea.

We could have been anybody, but the people are like that here. They are just so friendly and welcoming. They want to know where you are from. They are interested in people rather than materialistic things. So I said to Marilyn that this was a wonderful place, that the scenery was fantastic and the locals, if they were all like that, were so warm.

We were here for the summer when this job came up, and I was in two minds about whether to go for it. I was 30 and I thought I wouldn't have any chance because I was so young. But I discovered that the previous head had been appointed at about the same age, so I went for it.

By that time it was 1984 and I'd been coming up and down every year since 1979, but there were still some surprises round the corner. I hadn't realised just how important education is to the people here. On the mainland, you get a percentage of children for whom education is very important, who want to further themselves, to go on to tertiary education. But here, that percentage is much, much higher.

It is really very refreshing to go into a class where the children are keen and geared up to be taught. And you do teach them, rather than police them, which is what we had to do in some classes on the mainland. Discipline is not a problem.

The families are very keen that the children do well in school, and you get real support from them. If you called a parents' night in the south of Scotland, you would only get a small percentage of parents turning up, whereas here it is a small percentage who don't turn up.

It is a fantastic place to bring up children. It really is. When he is older, I would have no fear of Ross wandering up the village and speaking to people because everybody would keep an eye on him. He would know by that time not to speak to strangers, but that the people in the community are not strangers.

The quality of life is very, very good. There is little crime. Any crime is usually alcohol-related – people getting drunk and doing something silly like driving a car off the road. And there is great community spirit. To give you an example: when I came here at first, I was taken out fishing and I mentioned how much I like shellfish. The following week a bag of crabs turned up on the doorstep. Completely free. They were just there for me to help myself.

If you have a talent, they expect you to use that talent within the community. So people who go shellfishing, when they have a surplus, spread it around. And I spread my talent by taking classes at night.

But, for somebody like me, there are disadvantages to living here. I came from the mainland where I had a fairly sporty social life. I had been used to sports centres and swimming pools being close at hand, and I really do miss playing squash or volleyball, and meeting a lot of people of my own age and interests, or being able to go to the theatre or cinema, or having an Indian meal when I fancy it without having to make it.

Having said that, the social life here in the school is very good throughout the winter term because we have things on every night. I find that my evenings are full. Also, the main Hebridean social activity is conversation and there is a fairly open house policy. You can go to anybody's home any night and just sit and have a ceilidh. That's very nice, although, in spite of having been here for several years, I still find inviting myself into other people's houses a bit difficult. I don't do it as much as I think they would like me to because I still have that reticence, that in-built training that you should be invited before you barge in the door. But there are lots of evenings when I just feel like leaving work behind and going to visit people, and when I get that urge, I do it.

I must admit that I enjoy the Sundays here in that you know that you can have a quiet, relaxing time. I wouldn't like to be seen to be breaking the Sabbath and upsetting the code of conduct that locals go by – I wouldn't make a noise outside or hang out washing. On the other hand, in my own home, I get on with things that I want to do and I would be upset if anybody came in and told me that I shouldn't be doing something.

I'm from the west of Scotland and I still have my roots very much tied there. I enjoy the culture of the Hebrides and the Hearachs. I enjoy it for what it is. I like listening to them sing and tell stories. I like it, but I can't go overboard on it because I'm from a different background. I'm always wary of people who come in adopting everything. I question what's wrong with their own cultural background. So, yes, I grasp it as much as I want to grasp it, but I won't pretend to be completely, 100 per cent, won over. I won't cut off my own roots. I don't want to do that, and never will.

Sue Galbraith

Arinagour, Coll

Sue Galbraith first came to Coll through her friendship with a daughter of the Stewart family who were then, and had been for over a century previously, the local "lairds". That was in 1981. The following year, they offered her a seasonal job running a cafe; she accepted, and has lived on the island ever since.

Born and brought up in Worcestershire, she had spent almost all of her adult years working in different parts of Scotland. Coll impressed her with "its beauty and solitude" (around 130 people on an island 13 miles by four), and what she saw as a simpler and healthier way of life. She felt that this was somewhere she could settle. She fell in love with Neil, a local man who was the son of a farmer. They married and have their home in Arinagour.

In 1985, aged 32 and discontented with the job she was in, Sue turned her photography hobby into a business with the help of the Government's Enterprise Allowance Scheme. The venture flourished. Under her maiden name of Sue Anderson, she produces postcards and calendars of the inner and outer isles, Orkney and Shetland.

Our conversation wandered onto the subject of Hebridean men.

If you want the truth, I think they're real men – particularly in the physical sense. A lot of them are male chauvinist pigs, but I think they are very masculine. Within the family they have been brought up to see themselves in more of a traditional role than perhaps a lot of men in today's society on the mainland. The women have always done the domestic chores; and the boys have always worked outside, helping their fathers with the tough outdoor work. They've never really had the opportunity of becoming a modern man like a lot of men on the mainland where things like role reversal go on.

Sometimes I think that they've missed out on the understanding of new woman. They don't understand how this new woman has evolved. And equally they don't understand – and I'm sure they look down on – a lot of mainland men. They don't see these men as being very masculine because of this role reversal.

Living in Coll, in this environment, and doing the work that I do, I can't go out in my best make-up, in flowing skirts, or smart suits to run up and down hills taking photographs – sometimes in howling gales and horizontal rain. You can't look your feminine best in a job like that. But I like to try in certain situations. And I love a man to pull out a chair for me and open a door for me, and treat me like a lady. But, with the upbringing I've had, I also expect equality in a relationship.

I think it's more difficult for the Hebridean man to come to terms with making a relationship or a marriage work with a person from the outside. But I think that challenge is half the fun.

Island men have obviously mixed with, and met, and married people from the mainland and I think they are learning, but a lot of them are finding it difficult because old habits die hard. Some of them have strange ideas about keeping the woman under the thumb and they have great expectancies of what sort of mother their wives should be and how the children should be brought up. I don't know if you ever saw *The Bridal Path* where Bill Travers was sent off to hunt for a wife on the mainland and she had to have certain attributes...

I think that Hebridean men are certainly some of the most handsome in Britain. And they've got a charm. A lot of them have this mischievous glint in the eye, and a boyish charm. They have something about them, generally speaking, that is very attractive. I think it might have something to do with the fact that, for most, their work takes them outside into the harsh environment in all weather. I think that their characters and their physical features evolve around working outside, whether it's at farming or fishing. I think this gives them a much fresher, more rugged complexion and makes them much bigger and more masculine looking than a lot of young men on the mainland. Also, they don't have the same stresses and strains working in the islands. They don't have to worry about catching a train or missing a bus or queuing up for hours in a jam, or missing deadlines. They have different stresses and strains: those connected with the weather.

I think that they have a tolerant impatience of mainland men. That's a contradiction, I know, but I've thought about this. They obviously meet the ones that come to the islands – mostly as tourists – and they tolerate them and they learn what they can from them. They certainly don't mind learning from them and gleaning information about how they live, but I think they are also a bit impatient with the type of man that is being produced over there. They can't quite understand where basic masculinity went wrong.

I've mentioned some good points about them, but I also want to say some of the negative things about them. They're very irresponsible. I think that generally speaking, their boyish, mischievous attitude towards work and towards women and play stays with them through life and I think a lot of them don't ever mature very well. They're terribly irresponsible and I think a lot of this comes through in some of their social habits. A lot of them, when they marry and settle down and have a family, think that they can just be how they were before but with the wife and family at home providing that little bit of security and stability. I don't think they pull their weight in a marriage or a family relationship. I'm talking here in general about my generation. However, things are changing.

But you can't help but like them. They're likeable rogues and a great bunch of characters who would never hesitate to help you if you were in trouble.

Neil and I married down in England – which, on reflection, was a mistake. We should have got married here. I had left home when I was in my late teens and I quite soon found myself working in Scotland. I never did like where I grew up – 68 miles from the sea, in a quite industrial area of the Midlands – and I felt that Scotland was my home. That was where my roots were. My great-grandfather came from the east coast of Scotland and had moved down to the north of England, which was a very sorry mistake in my opinion.

You've heard about how an English wedding is so different to a traditional Scottish wedding. I think that, having been here for so many years before I married, I would have fitted in better to a Scottish wedding. And my relations would have fitted in better up here than Neil and his family fitted into an English wedding. The celebrations stopped very early and it was all very proper and formal. Up here it would have been a much more relaxed, longer, enjoyable affair with all the community joining in rather than just a chosen few.

But, anyway, that's just my opinion. English weddings are not very inspiring. They're like the English New Year. Hogmanay is just nothing down there.

New Year in Coll is very much what you make it. Traditionally for Neil, it has always been a time of taking quite a few days off work – indeed, it could be stretched to over a week or two – and spending Hogmanay night at home to bring in the lump of coal and then go first-footing, and visiting every person on the island, more or less. And when in Rome... So I've joined him for many years. It's very much a case of visiting people with good wishes and a few drams, and putting the world to right, and doing a lot of walking.

Having lived in Scotland for many years, I had an idea it would be like that here. But I've never met people with such a serious attitude to it. You visit all these houses and if it takes a week, it takes a week. A very sociable occasion.

I would never, ever go south of the Border for Hogmanay now, and haven't done so for many years. Christmas, yes. But not Hogmanay.

Christmas is quite miserable here. [Laughter]. That's from an English person's point of view. If you spend it with a family, you might get what I would call a good Sunday dinner. A few trimmings if there are children in the house – crackers and this and that. There's not the whole build-up of hanging up the stockings, and the presents round the tree, and the lights, and the decorations all over the house, and carol singing, and Father Christmas: the sort of thing I was brought up with down in England. Down there, there's a great build-up to it. But Christmas here is just like one grand Sunday afternoon ceremony, and then New Year comes in with much more excitement and enthusiasm.

Has anyone mentioned the drinking on the islands? The drinking on all the islands, in my opinion, is excessive. There is no one island that is worse than any other. I think that they all have a major problem. A lot of social things are revolved around drinking: if it's a dance, there's a bar; if it's a barbecue on the beach, there's always booze; if it's visiting old folk, you're offered a wee refreshment. And I think this custom of having alcohol with basically every social occasion has got out of hand. Though I'm not a teetotaller myself.

One idea I have as to the reason for this – although I by no means consider myself to have the answer to everything or anything – is the weather and the type of work people do. If the weather's bad it's a hard struggle to get basic things done: to replace the slates on the roof, or keep the outbuildings and stores wind and watertight at the height of a storm, or to get that beast to market, or to keep that beast alive. I think the environment has a lot to do with the fact that traditionally, on a bad day, people will sometimes have a dram because that will make them feel better. It will lift them up and help them face the problems.

If they've completed a particularly hard task – rounding up a whole flock of sheep when the dogs won't work, or putting a couple of difficult cows into a trailer – they might have a dram. It's like a celebration of a hard job of work being done.

Traditionally, it has always been that islanders have enjoyed a dram. But I think the environment – battling with the elements – is part of what makes the problem. I mean, when you're up to your knees in shit and the rain's coming down in sheets of horizontal force, a dram is really the first thing you want when you get into the dry by the fire. I've been in that situation myself when I've been out on the hill lambing. [On the Stewart estate.] And it's a way of relaxing and letting off steam. The use of leisure time up here is not as constructive as on the mainland. The opportunities for sport and other interesting pursuits don't exist. And I think, for some people, drinking becomes a habit – a habit which eventually gets out of hand.

I worked for Project Trust [see page 131] for two and a half years. They bring an interesting bunch of youngsters between the ages of 17 and 19 here every winter for four-day assessment courses, and during those four days, amongst other things, they have to make observations about the community and the way of life. They used to write a little essay on what they thought of the island and her people. And it always struck me that nine times out of 10, they got a very romantic idea about life here. It's only by staying and living as part of the community that you realise that there's nothing much romantic about the islands. It's just a figment of the imagination. People don't really understand how difficult it is to make ends meet. You have to be quite strong to survive.

Rebecca MacKay

Oskaig, Raasay

A 15-minute ferry crossing takes the traveller from Sconser on Skye to Raasay, a thin strip of an island – just 13 miles by three – which is home to a population of 150. From the pier at East Suisnish, I followed a road lined with lush vegetation – rhododendron bushes, woodland, and colourful domestic gardens – to Oskaig where Rebecca MacKay lives with her husband Calum on their small croft.

Born in 1945 of a Raasay mother, Rebecca was brought up in Dundonald in Ayrshire. She moved to Portree to teach English in the local school in 1976, and then to Raasay to marry Calum, a local, six years later. He is employed by the Forestry Commission and she does bed and breakfast in their modern bungalow.

No sooner had I switched on the tape recorder and asked her about the way of life, than we were suddenly and rudely interrupted by a military aircraft zooming overhead.

It's very peaceful and calm, except when you get something like that. That can be very frightening. I heard a lady saying on the radio yesterday that planes fly so low where she lives that she automatically ducks. I have done that a couple of times here. I have actually cowered with the noise. Sometimes they fly from the east side of the island roughly north west. Sometimes they just go up and down over the water here. They have been asked to avoid the area when it's lambing time but they say they can't just work out when everyone's lambing time is. And if a human being gets upset, dear knows what it's doing to the animals.

Socially, if you want cinemas and theatres and all that, this is not the place to be. But if you enjoy speaking to people, then it is. In the summertime there are dances, and at New Year there may be a dance or two or sometimes a ceilidh. But most of the ceilidhs are still impromptu ceilidhs. People will just arrive and that will be you for the night, singing or sitting talking about what's gone on through the day, what's happened in the past, what happened hundreds of years ago.

If it's a holiday period, the dances will be fairly busy, but then there tends to be an awful lot of outsiders and that does change the atmosphere in the hall. Before, it would be predominantly Raasay people and Raasay people home on holiday. But now, with the island being more available to outsiders, there is definitely a change in attitude. For example, sometimes you get people trying to play disco music which just isn't part of Highland culture at all. A few years ago you would get people of maybe 50 or 60 years of age. But I have noticed that they are disappearing because of the change in the style of the dances. It's not so much fun any more for locals.

However, the pursuit of such worldly pleasure does not meet with universal approval on the island. Raasay's two churches are the Free Presbyterian Church of Scotland, and the Free Church of Scotland. Most of the natives, particularly the elderly, are devoutly religious and there are those who regard dances as ungodly. The Sabbath is strictly observed...

Traditionally, dinner is prepared on a Saturday night. The shoes are cleaned and the men shave. Only work of necessity – feeding the animals – is done on a Sunday. We go to church, read the Bible, and eat. I'm not sure all people live like that, but the older generation most certainly do.

If you accept other aspects of life, then you accept the religious way too. You can't pick out the bits that you like and the bits that you don't like. A lot of people come to the island to get away from it all but they bring their values with them. They try to change the way of life and they certainly do not respect that of the people here. Sunday is the busiest day of the week on the road. On Sunday I counted nine cars, one after the other, all going north. They come from the outdoor centre and let holiday houses. Local people feel very angry about the lack of respect shown to the values that the islanders have.

I think maybe visitors don't realise just how offensive they are. I don't think people would worry too much if somebody went out for a walk. A nice wee quiet walk wouldn't do anybody any harm. Or for that matter, they could sit outside on a sunny day. But not racing off in cars going here, there and everywhere. You need a day of rest. Why not have it when everyone else is having it?

To the Raasay islanders, the Church is extremely important. It's very much part of their life. It's a part of their life that is with them day and night, year in, year out. The whole family worship morning and night-time every day in most homes, reading a part from the Bible, singing part of a psalm, saying a prayer.

There is a prayer meeting on a Wednesday night and the Raasay folk will not organise anything to take place during that. After it, yes. During it, no. If you don't go to church, then you don't do anything during that period.

It is very, very easy for an incomer to be accepted if you are prepared to become part of the community. There is a couple along the road there – they came from Largs – and they are as much part of Raasay life as anybody else is. But there are others who do not integrate. They bring their lifestyles with them. They won't observe the values of the people and they will never, ever be part of Raasay life. They're just totally distanced from the local people.

I read in a newspaper clipping not so long ago a letter written by a fellow who comes here on holiday and he called the people "joyless." He doesn't know them. I've never met such happy people. I mean, they may not go to pubs and get drunk but they have a joy and a happiness in their lives, and a friendliness and a hospitality that you just don't find anywhere else. I think the people are extremely happy.

The islanders are placid. You don't find people physically fighting here in the way that you do elsewhere, although you're bound to have disputes – this would be Utopia if people lived together without falling out. You get the usual disagreements about bits and pieces, but nothing major.

There is a lack of crime. No murders. No housebreaking. But then again, in the summertime you don't know who's around and you do tend to get some weird people appearing. One year there was a guy going about with a machete. Another year we had a group of so-called survivalists over from England who fired some sort of shotgun into vehicles up at the fank. You do get that sort of upset periodically. But most people are law abiding.

When I was a youngster and we were leaving, I used to cry from when we got on the boat at Raasay pier until we got to Kyle where I could see the last of Raasay in the distance. I used to howl. It was really awful. And when I go away from home now, I want back again. Maybe I'm odd but three days away from home and that's quite enough for me.

Iain Angus and Murdina Murray

Coll, Lewis

In the early hours of New Year's morning, 1919, Lewis was struck by a devastating disaster. HM Yacht Iolaire, loaded with 260 naval ratings and a crew of 24, hit a ridge of rock known as the Beasts of Holm close to the entrance to Stornoway harbour. The servicemen were returning from the war, many for the first time since 1914. While relatives and friends met up on board ship, in houses all over the island their loved ones prepared for the homecoming.

Only 79 survived the wreck. Mostly they did so either by swimming for shore or by clambering along a lifeline which one man had managed to secure between the Iolaire and dry land. The rest drowned in the icy black water or were dashed on the rocks in their attempts to reach safety.

The close-knit island community was overwhelmed by grief. James Shaw Grant notes in his book, Discovering Lewis and Harris, that Iain Crichton Smith in some of his poems "more than half a century after the event, has grappled with some of the profound philosophical and religious questions such a disaster, at such a time, raises for a community which sees the hand of God in everything."

For generations, Hebridean men have looked to the sea for their livelihood or as a means to make their way in the world. It has been a dangerous ally.

Of the 79 men who lived to tell the tale of the Iolaire disaster, two were still alive when I visited Lewis in October 1990. One, Donald Murray – who had also survived being torpedoed on more than one occasion during the war – was living in North Tolsta at the age of 96. I called on his son and daughter-in-law, Iain Angus and Murdina Murray, at their home in the village of Coll. Like his father, Iain Angus – now semi-retired from his fishing boat, Comrade – knows how it feels to have the sea's jaws snapping at his heels.

I was born in North Tolsta. I married up here 31 years ago. I was fishing all my life very near. I started in 1942 as a 14-year-old boy. I left school at the summer holidays and I wasn't 14 till August, but I just managed to get clear by inches.

It was the first thing you were thinking of at school – the sea, going to sea. Everyone in my class – I think bar two, one became a teacher, the other a policeman – went to sea. To the merchant navy most of them.

So I went on my father's boat as a cook in the September.

You had to coil tarry rope all night long. I was seasick and the old boys used to say, "Go and put on a pan of herring." You couldn't get anybody to do that kind of job today. And that was at £3-10-0 a week. Working night and day.

We lost that boat in 1952 in Loch Claidh at the border to Harris. That was with a gale of south-east wind. Something happened to the engine. The boat drifted on the rocks. We all jumped ashore. This was at 2 o'clock in the morning on the 7th of January. Pitch dark and solid snow.

There was nothing in the area for miles and miles. We started to walk and we knew that there was one [uninhabited] house on the Lewis side of Loch Seaforth, opposite Maaruig in Harris. But we didn't have a clue which way we were going. We made an L kind of a thing. So we reached that house at about half past three in the afternoon – if we had made a short cut it wouldn't have taken us so long.

There was a small black stove in the place – the old type – and there were bits of wood and things like that lying around so we put on a fire. We got a sheep and killed it. We were starving.

We were in that house until 10 o'clock at night. There were

people in the houses across the loch in Maaruig and we had a torch, so we started flashing the torch across.

They came over with a boat and got us. And oh, we got plenty of attention. Plenty food. Plenty everything. Even clothes if we wanted. I don't know about the older ones: did they take a change of clothes? But we never bothered.

We hired a bus from Harris. It was three o'clock in the morning when we reached home. They didn't know at home that anything had happened to us. They thought we were alright. There were no wirelesses then on the boats.

After that, I went to the east coast, to Peterhead, and I fished there right up to the time we got our own boat again – well, I made a couple of trips in the merchant navy and then went back to the fishing. I was about 10 years on the east coast. I was leaving here in March and I wouldn't be back again until September. Then you would get a fortnight at home and go to the Yarmouth fishing. That's the carry on we had then.

It was while he was based on a Peterhead boat that Iain Angus had another narrow escape. That was in 1960, just a few weeks after he and Murdina married.

There were three of us from the island on this boat and the skipper came down this Friday and said they were going home that weekend and one of us could go home to Lewis while the other two looked after the boat in Ullapool.

The one that was going home would be picked up on the Tuesday morning in Stornoway.

There was this young fellow – I was young at the time too, but this fellow was younger than me – and two of us were in the hold filling the baskets of herring. And the skipper said he was going over to the office to get the wages and when he came back, whoever was going ashore was to be ready.

Well this young fellow said to me, "It's you that's going ashore."

"Me?", I said, "I was never so lucky as that."

"Ah," he said, "I'll do the matches and when I give them to you, you pick this one."

So I knew then it was me that was going.

When the skipper came back from the office, he said who was there but the skipper of the Fertility, another Peterhead boat, and he had said that one of his crew was at home at a funeral. If the boat I was on would take this guy on from Ullapool on the Monday, I could go aboard the Fertility in Stornoway on the Monday and the two of us would change over whenever the boats met again. So that was alright.

So away we went on the Monday. We went by Tiumpan Head there and I went to bed, reading a paper. But being on a new boat, I couldn't sleep seeing it wasn't my own usual bed. I was saying to myself that the wind was getting up. She started rolling and jumping about. I went up and looked out of the galley and there was a gale of wind on then.

We went as far north as Cellar Head, very near at Ness there, and I heard the skipper speaking on the radio and he said he was going to turn back. It was getting too much.

I came up again when we were coming to Tiumpan Head – I was up and down like that, just fed up – and then I went back to this bunk and started reading something. About three-quarters of an hour after that: *bang*. That was us full speed on the rocks.

Oh, the lights went out. Everything went black. So we got a torch and went down below. The water was gushing in then. Nothing we could do. There were no life-rafts – none of the new type of life-rafts – just a small boat. One wave of that and a small boat would have been in a thousand pieces on the rocks.

This was sometime at the end of January or in February, and we had got married in December, and one of the boys was saying to me, "Well, I think Murdina is going to hold a record for the time she was married."

"Oh," I said, "Don't tell me that."

Ah, but he went hysterical.

"Well," I was saying to myself, "If it's going to happen, it's going to happen. What are you going to do?" Getting hysterical like that wasn't going to do any good.

Now, it was an air-start engine. With engines now it's electric – batteries – but it was air that was starting this. But she wouldn't start. Not a bit. This was at 11 o'clock at night. Dark as tar and a force nine gale right against the rocks. Lumps of sea coming down and battering the boat against the rocks.

So the driver came up this time and said, "There's only one puff left. I don't know..."

The skipper said, "Well try that puff. It might work. Who knows?"

This was the last chance. We couldn't put out a mayday because the wireless went off when the lights went out. If we had the wireless we could have shouted something, but no one would get near you in those conditions.

So he tried this puff. Away she went. But, here you are, we knew she was badly damaged. So we put the pumps on. There were two pumps aboard.

She went out astern. The water was gushing in then. So he put her ahead. The way she was going through the sea, the planks must be tightening against you with the pressure of the sea. So we shouted to him to give her more power. Well, the more power he was giving her, the tighter. But at long last she was holding her own. The pumps were holding the sea that was coming in.

Anyway, coming in at the light there in Stornoway the skipper asked me, seeing I was a local, what was the best place to go because this thing was going to sink once we stopped.

"Well," I said, "It's number two in front of the Cally there." That's where we used to beach the boats.

She was very near full when we got her in because he had to slow her down coming in to approach the quay. The fire engine came down right away and kept her dry until the sea went out and she was beached and we patched her for taking her home.

In 1963, Iain Angus took Comrade home for the first time, through the Pentland Firth.

When we left Macduff, they told us, "Now, that boat's new. Don't put the engine up past 800 revs for the first week or so until it works itself in."

There was no sense in going into the Pentland Firth until you had the tide running with you. The tide would be as fast as your boat if it was coming against you. Now, if it was with you, you could stop the engine and go through the Firth very near just as fast.

But, what happened was, the tide was against us. We were too early. We went right into it and the wind was from the south, and with the two things coming together we didn't know where the waves were coming from. In a normal heavy sea you can dodge the boat up – the waves come in one after the other from the same direction.

We didn't know what to do. I thought, "This is it. We've had it."

But once the tide changed, the sea went as calm as that floor. It was just the current and the wind, and we couldn't get out of it.

I think that was the biggest sea I've ever seen in my life. Forty/fifty feet waves.

I always had a good nerve. I saw people going very, very frightened when they were thinking things were bad. But I was never afraid at sea. I am more afraid here when there's a gale of wind on this house. You wouldn't think the boats would weather what they go through. You would say it was impossible. But if you handle them right, they're like lifeboats. No bother.

I suppose I was 46 years at sea and at the end of the time, my legs were starting to go – hardening of the arteries or whatever it is. So I'm not missing it as much as I was. I've been away all the time very near since we got married, so I'm enjoying being at home now. We've got 40 sheep and I potter around all the time. There are eight acres of croft here.

Like all women whose husbands take their living from the deep,

Murdina knows how it feels to spend anxious hours listening to the howling wind. Iain Angus may be safely ashore, but his wife's anxiety goes on over her son Iain, who is now skipper on Comrade, and others like him.

I've had all my life with the sea. All my life I've been practically on my own bringing up the children. But I was young then. I took things in my stride. Nowadays, I seem to worry more and more. I understand the gales more. Of course, you pray a lot. When there's a gale or anything, you're forever praying that everybody will be safe. Prayer helps. You turn to God a lot.

When you're young, you hear the gales but you don't realise how dangerous they are. And I had great faith in him. When he was with a boat, I would think, "Well, nothing will happen. He's been at it now for years."

But I'm not as young as I used to be. When there's a gale on, the pressure goes sky-high worrying about them. I ask, "Do you think they'll be out tonight?"

"*No*, they're not out," he'll say.

Sometimes they are, but they don't tell me.

Sonia and John Bidwell

Borreraig, Skye

Sonia and John Bidwell are well-practised in being incomers. During their married life they have lived in London, Sussex, Suffolk, and Norfolk.

While on holiday in Skye in the early 1980s (on their first visit to Scotland), they spotted an empty house on a disused croft in the north west of the island. Both were attracted by what John describes as "the spaces between the people. The fact that people are close enough to react as neighbours, but there are never crowds. There is still a community."

Being self-employed in arboriculture, he felt he could do just as well in Skye as he had in the south. Their two daughters were at transitional stages in their lives anyway – one at university, the other about to change schools. It seemed like an ideal time to move and by the summer of 1983 they were in their new home, although it was another 15 months before the croft was assigned to them.

Both have adapted happily and with sensitivity to the local way of life. But there were problems in the early days.

Sonia: Our younger daughter was not successful in adjusting. When we came here there was an anti-English atmosphere on the school bus. She didn't go under, but she became very good at swearing in Gaelic and she came up with fists and hair flying. I have talked to people about it since and because there are more incomers on the bus now, it has improved. Also, the school did try to sort it out. I think it was just a particular phase. There was an influx of incomers. I think the local children felt threatened really.

And although the school is very good, there is old-fashioned discipline and she'd come from an open-plan, do-your-own-project, kind of school. It was very hard for her. She never really settled.

However, the adult population lived up to all of the Bidwells' expectations of Highland neighbourliness and hospitality. John does estimating and other work for a construction company on a self-employed basis and his vivacious wife has become the crofter on their six acres of land. Neither were agricultural greenhorns. He had worked on and around farms in England; she had some veterinary training before they married. But they needed practical advice from local people...

John: In crofting matters, if you ask for anybody's help, you will get it. Unquestioning.

Sonia: Everyone was very good. I couldn't have managed without our next door neighbour over at the post office. He took me under his wing really. He taught me how to do things and then left me to get on with them. He taught me how to shear. The first year, he had me hold the sheep and he sheared it. The second year, I sheared the sheep while he held it. And in the third year, I was on my own. He helped me in every way.

My life has done a complete circle. I have come back to doing the things I enjoyed as a child – I'm out of doors most of the day working on the croft, and I've become much more church-orientated. I had quite a religious upbringing, but then I kind of drifted in and out. Then, coming up here, I found the church community marvellous. I go to the Church of Scotland. It's very pleasant going to a well-attended church. I thoroughly enjoy it. I went in Norfolk, but there would be six old ladies and the local brigadier, and that was it. Our older daughter and I used to ring the bells and then rush down from the church tower and she'd rush to play the organ and I'd hand out the hymn books. It was a bit like one of those travelling circuses where one minute you're taming lions and the next you're serving ice cream. But here, the church is full and everybody knows what they're doing. Also, I like the Church of Scotland. I have been to the Free Church and I like it occasionally, but it's just so different. It's a controversial subject, but I don't find it very uplifting.

Yes, I must say, I didn't realise the church would come to mean so much to me.

The island way of life came to mean even more to the Bidwells when, not long after they moved to Skye, Sonia's mother died. She had lived with them for years and they found their neighbours' reactions to their loss a great source of comfort.

John: People here have a very healthy attitude to death. They mourn. Death is made into a ceremony and as many people as possible are involved in it. It is a major rite of passage – not only for the person concerned, but for the whole family, for the friends, for the friends of friends. There are none of these 'No Flowers' or 'Family Only Please' requests. A death is an occasion and it must be marked. This is the only place I have ever worked where the entire workforce will go off for two hours in the middle of the day to attend a funeral.

Sonia: And the boss wouldn't think of questioning it.

My mother died here at home and when she was dying, the whole township came to visit her. They didn't sit there looking terribly mournful. They chatted away to her perfectly normally. And when she died all the able men of the township came to the funeral and they all carried her coffin. And this was amazing to us. We had never experienced anything like it. Then, after the service, instead of the mourners getting into their cars and disappearing, everyone spoke to us. And this helps the grief because afterwards people aren't avoiding you and wondering what to say – you've done all that and you can pick up the threads of life.

John: Death is faced. It is spoken about. It is not regarded as something rather indecent. And there is none of this American idea that we are all immortal, that none of us must ever grow old. You can grow old gracefully here because old people have a position in the community. They can go to all the functions for example. In suburban areas entertainment tends to be stratified: teenagers, 24-35-year-olds, and so on up to pensioners. Each group having its own form of entertainment. The great thing here is that if you have, say, the Crofters Union annual dance, everybody goes. From the youngest up to the oldest. All have a good time and all fit in somewhere.

Old people very rarely feel rejected by the community. They're an important part of it. And so, when it comes to death, it's not an anonymous person from an old people's home that has gone. It is someone who is known and loved.

Major Colin Campbell

Flodda (Benbecula)

There wasn't much time as I hopped around the islands to get out of the car to sniff the heavenly tang of the seaweed, or feel the breeze in my face, or listen to the silence. When you visit Major Colin Campbell, all of this is unavoidable. He lives on the tiny island of Flodda, which is linked by causeway to the north-eastern edge of Benbecula. On reaching Flodda, the road deteriorates into a rough track and then disappears, so getting out to walk is the only option.

I was gazing around uncertainly on a late October day when the Major appeared over a rise with his two collies to show me around. We admired the scenery and the seals basking on the rocks waiting for the tide to lift them off. Chivalrously he insisted on carrying my briefcase.

His home is an old croft house. Operatic music drifted through from the kitchen when he went off to fetch tea (China) and cakes. Meanwhile, I savoured the crowded atmosphere of the small sitting-room. Portraits of his ancestors – mostly men in red military tunics – lined the walls. There were old decanters, a framed black and white photograph of the Princess Royal, a failed experiment with mussels in a tank, a regimental drum, a sword. Somehow, the effect refused to be incongruous.

When he entered the army, Colin became the sixth generation of his family to do so. Born in 1934 to parents of Highland descent, he was brought up in England. He joined the Black Watch after public school and served for 20 years. On leaving in 1970, he spent a year sailing to the Canary Islands and back. It was during that time that his brother – also an army man – discovered the croft on Flodda and thought it just right for the outward bound centre the two had been planning to set up in their retirement.

For various reasons the centre didn't get off the ground, but Colin now works around 300 acres of croft – some on Flodda, but most on a neighbouring peninsula. He never married, and lives alone.

After the causeway was built, the road gradually came further and further out until it reached where it is now. I'm not convinced I want it to come to the house yet. What do you think? I have a little buffer. If you're at the end of the road, you tend to get people coming out for a drive. Now, it would be horrid to think that they shouldn't come out, but it would make a difference somehow.

I think people think I was against the causeway. Well I wasn't really. But I was in the position of not really caring too much whether it was there or not. Whereas I think locally they wanted it, so I waded in with them and supported it. I'm very happy now. It makes my life much more comfortable, just as it does for everyone else. But for them it was a much more urgent matter. And I think that's where incomers can be on tricky ground: if they like things the way they find them and they prevent development happening. But the question of the road coming to the house doesn't benefit anyone else so it's not quite the same thing.

When I came to Flodda, I was delighted to find that my neighbours were so extremely kind and hospitable and put me right on all sorts of things to do with crofting; and we've always been on excellent terms. They gave me a great deal of help on things like peat cutting. To this day we help each other with various things like the dipping and the shearing. For example, I have neighbours on Grimsay who have the other big croft on Rossinish and on Friday I'm meant to be going to help them to do the dipping. Then, on a day yet to be chosen, they'll come with a gang to do the same for me.

I nearly left the army a lot earlier. I'm quite heavily involved at the moment in this business of trying to save the Scottish regiments, and they did a similar sort of business in the 1960s and I wrote to the papers while still a serving officer and there were rumblings about courts martial and things like that and I thought then that if I did have to go, what I would probably like to do would be crofting.

So I did quite a lot of investigation into crofting then. The idea of crofting – sharing common work, and the self-sufficiency part of it, providing it wasn't too cranky and in crofting it isn't – always appealed to me. But I didn't have any experience of shearing sheep by hand and that sort of thing.

Also, I've always been interested in Gaelic. I had tried to learn before I came to Flodda, but not very successfully, I'm afraid. I think it is one of the more difficult languages to learn. I learned Russian when I was in the army with much greater ease. I went on a course to Sabhal Mor Ostaig on Skye after I came here and I greatly enjoyed it, and it was a great help, but I'm still not much better at talking other than passing the time of day. I can understand the Gaelic on the radio quite well. I listen to that, but I find it much more difficult in conversation at the sheep fank.

I do attempt to speak it but I haven't been as bold as I should have. I used to try and spend the first five or 10 minutes in Gaelic when I went to neighbours but I could see that it was actually a burden for them when we wanted to discuss what had been going on in the day to have me stumbling along. So gradually, I'm afraid, we discontinued that. But one thing I like is that when we are dipping or shearing or doing these communal things, they treat me more or less as one of them and will continue to speak in Gaelic without lapsing into English for my benefit, which is a thing I greatly appreciate. It helps me too to pick up words and expressions. I think they're disappointed that my Gaelic hasn't improved, just as I am.

I think how you fit in depends on your attitude. If incomers are prepared to join in the community whole-heartedly then people are extremely welcoming. But I think if they try and maintain a different social circle – and there are enough of them nowadays to do that – then it is much more difficult for both of the communities to join together. There are sometimes things like battles in the pub between the local young and the army young who come over from Germany on courses. [To the missile range on Benbecula]. But on the whole there's very little of that. The army are very much self-contained and have their own clubs and things like that.

As an example of what I was saying about fitting in, I think I found it rather difficult to start with because although I wasn't a gunner, the army here very kindly said I could be an honorary member of the mess and go to their functions. And I did, for perhaps a year or so. And then I began to realise that it was actually rather difficult because perhaps some of the waiters were my neighbours and there was a little bit, I thought, of a feeling in the camp then – I hope it isn't there now – of a them and us attitude. They would talk slightly disparagingly about the natives and I felt that I had got to decide: am I a crofter or am I a retired army officer? I didn't see that I could really honestly be in both positions. So I think I'm still technically an honorary member but I haven't been there for many years now. I'm still on very good terms with them but I think they appreciate the thing as well – that you can't really be both.

So those are some thoughts on how incomers mix in. I think it does depend a huge amount on how they're prepared to help in the community. Are they aloof or do they join in? Do they address each other by Christian names? For example, I've always insisted that everyone call me by my Christian name since I came here. I don't think one could possibly have done otherwise.

I still consider myself as an incomer, as a guest in a sense. I'm very aware of that. I will never be an islander and I think we all accept that. But I go to their homes and I am treated as one of the family, and the same thing happens if they come here.

One of the great problems for young folk – of which I'm not including myself! – is that there is very little to do in the evenings. Just really the pub. So there is quite a lot of drinking done and I rather like my dram so we often have little sprees here and there at each other's houses. And they very kindly when they've had weddings and things like that invite me along. I've been to those of people I know. And funerals.

I feel as well accepted by them as one could possibly ever hope to be, and they're kindness itself. We swap birthday presents and things like that. I've had a rocket on the 'phone from some neighbours because I haven't been over to see them for so long. So I've promised I'll be going next week after dipping.

As I say, I still feel I'm a guest here but I do feel very much part of it in other ways. I love their music and their singing and dancing.

You either love the music or you hate it, it seems to me. And it always intrigued me – long before I came here. Probably people would shoot you down for saying this, but I have a feeling that there may be something genetic in that particular type of music. If I haven't heard it for some time, the hair on the back of my neck stands up. Yes, it seems to me to be part of one's make-up. It's rather hard to describe but it's something that you feel is part of you and I would hate now to be without it.

I piped a bit myself. There are a lot of pipers here. My neighbour is a piper and a very good box player, so we have wonderful ceilidhs, long into the dawn sometimes in winter.

I don't find it lonely here at all. I was always a little bit of a loner, I suppose. I liked to get away when I could on my own. Funnily enough, loneliness and boredom are two things one never suffers from here. I've got hundreds of projects I should be doing. I wanted to write up my sailing spree and that's been waiting for a very long time. I started a book which is meant to be slightly taking apart the conservation lobby – the more earnest side of it – because they have been seen as being overbearing and tiresome by many folk in the islands. I think relationships are improving now but there was a time when perfectly innocent things that crofters used to do – like shooting the odd cormorant for their supper at certain times of the year – have now become illegal. And they haven't been allowed to do certain improvements so that the corncrakes will survive. Now, I'm not against corncrakes, but I think these people gave the impression that they were much more concerned about feathered friends than the two-footed inhabitants of the islands.

There are always things one ought to be doing, like making creels, and I've always been rather interested in family history so I've got huge quantities of genealogical tables and things waiting to be sorted out one day. And somehow, there's never time for it all.

I don't greatly like this time of year – just when you realise that summer's away and you get a big storm and the ground changes colour and you realise that winter's on you. But once we actually get into it – say, perhaps, when the hour goes back – then it's a different life altogether. There's something rather nice about it because instead of having a lot of jobs inside that you ought to be doing, you've got a whole lot of jobs outside that you ought to be doing. But when it's dark at both ends of the day, you know that you can't do things like sorting roofs. So, in a sense, in the evening your conscience is relieved of any responsibilities of going outside. And therefore you are thrown on your own resources, and it's rather nice.

Of course, a very fortunate thing is the broadcasting from Radio nan Gaidheal. You can get very good programmes every evening. I think I might be lonely if I didn't have the wireless. I suppose I depend on that a great deal.

I hate the telephone and I'm afraid to say that if you try to ring me, you probably won't get an answer. I do use it – it's very handy for ringing out – but I always think that telephones ought to be slaves and not masters. I very frequently have it unswitched for hours at a time and people can't understand that.

I think it might be because I was at such beck and call in the army. I'd be called out in the middle of the night for an exercise or practice or something. It was just such a relief to get rid of all that, that I've now gone against it entirely. It seems to exercise a discipline on people and they feel they must answer. I have had people sitting here and the 'phone has rung and I didn't want to answer so I let it ring, and they have rushed up and answered it themselves.

I suppose that leads us on to a slight disadvantage to living here. One of the reasons perhaps I got fed up with the 'phone was that after I had been in here for a little bit, people would arrive without any warning on the ferry and they'd ring from Lochmaddy: "Ah, Colin. I haven't seen you for years. We're in Lochmaddy, the wife and I. Can we come and stay?"

If somebody rings up like that, I can never think of an excuse, so I have to say, "Oh yes. Of course." Anything worse than people arriving without any warning at all... I think people have taken the hint now. I haven't had that recently, but for the first few years it was a pain. I'd get hordes of people coming and they would think it tremendous fun to stay for two days but perhaps they didn't realise that somebody else had come the weekend before. And at that time too, the causeway wasn't there and everything had to be carried over in packs from the car.

So it was very nice to see people but you had this dilemma. It was an awful burden and also it stopped you getting on with things. They would say, "Oh, we'll join in." But very seldom were they in a position to join you in the sort of things that needed to be done.

Can he see himself living there in old age?

Well, I suppose I've always been rather fatalistic about that sort of thing. I take my fences as I come to them. It doesn't worry me really. If anything happens, something will turn up. It's not a thing that weighs on my mind at 3 o'clock in the morning.

Kate Ann MacLellan

Tigharry, North Uist

Kate Ann MacLellan was born in Tigharry in 1933, and has lived there all of her life. She is married to Tommy and has two sons, one of whom works the family croft.

I was brought up with my grandmother. She didn't have a croft. It was just a small cottar's house she had. A small thatched house. It had two bedrooms and a kitchen. Outside, we were drawing water from a well. We had no electricity. First of all, we had an oil lamp, then we went on to have a tilley lamp, and eventually, we had a gas light.

Tigharry is dying out now. There's hardly any of the old folk left and there's hardly any young ones growing up. I think there's only about one or two families with very young children here now. The school has closed.

The way of crofting is different. When I was growing up, the work was done with horses and ploughs. Now it's all done by tractors. Silage is becoming the thing. In my day it was scything. The men would be out scything and the women were binding after them. They were milking cows in those days, and they were doing butter and cheese, and feeding the calves from buckets. Nowadays nobody's milking and there's no cheese-making.

Up to two years ago, I was milking and I used to do butter and cheese – and I'd sell quite a bit of it as well – but I had to give that up owing to ill health. I used to help out a lot on the croft. I thought it was great working outside – being among the cattle, and getting the pleasure of milking and doing so many things with our own milk, and having the pleasure of giving some butter or crowdie away to people who were so keen on getting it.

There have been a lot of changes – regarding the crofting ways, and the old people dying away. We don't seem to know so much now. We should have been listening to more of what the old people had to tell us. In winter-time they used to gather round in the houses and have a wee blether together. My grandmother's house was always quite full in winter-time, and they talked about their young lives, and about what their work involved. I'm sure I didn't find it very interesting at the time, but I would be very interested to have all of that today.

My grandmother used to go down to the seashore and take a lot of dulses and seaweeds and things home and make different dishes with them. Nobody does that now. She used to take home winkles and cook them and put them into white sauce. Sometimes they were fried with oatmeal. Limpets were cooked and the juice that came off them was strained and put into bottles and used for medicine. And large white shells – I couldn't really tell you the proper names for them – she used to collect those. They were just empty shells which came up into the shingle and she would collect them and boil them and make lime water out of them. That was used for several things including worms in children.

She used to take home dulse, which was very sweet tasting. We'd eat it raw, or she would boil it in milk. And in February and March, there was another kind of weed which you just twirled round your finger to take it off the rock. I just can't remember very well the recipe for that, but I know it was washed several times to remove any sand and it was put into a three-legged cast iron pot, and she kept beating it with a wooden spoon until at last it was in liquid form when it was cooked. And that was drained and bottled and it had a lot of iron in it. So if you were run down or listless, it was used for that.

She was the same with plants. I'm very sad that I don't know the names of any of these plants or anything about them. I'm sure they are there yet and the same things could be done with them. They were made into ointments and liquids. There was one plant and if you had a fall and the sore wasn't cleaning out properly, she would get this plant out of the ground and you would warm it at the fire and it would get very soft, like silk. And it had like white strings in it, and you would pull the strings out, and it was just like velvet when you did that, and that would be put on the sore to draw the pus out of it.

She made cream with "old man's beard", as they called it. You get that off the rocks – on the ground, not at the shore. We used to put fresh home-made butter along with that and make a cream out of it which was for healing burns, and sunburn, and a lot of things.

It's one thing I regret very much: that I didn't take more interest in those things I saw her doing.

In the old days, you see, they didn't have medicines or anything. They were depending a lot on their knowledge. Maybe there were quite a few of them that could do all that, but I think some of them were wiser than others in these ways.

They paid a lot of attention to the sea and the sky. They would say to you that bad weather was on the way, or that it was going to settle down and be good weather. They seemed to be making a lot of use of their talents.

Say there was a very calm sea and all of a sudden it started changing and it became very rough. My grandmother would say, "There's bad weather on the way. That's the sea turning." And sure enough, there would be. If there was a bright sun and maybe instead of one sun, you were seeing two – they had a Gaelic name for that – that was a bad sign again. I never hear anybody nowadays saying things like that.

When my grandmother was putting down a hatching of eggs under a broody hen, she would go to the window if it was a bright sunny day and she would hold the egg with her hand above it and say, "This one is fertile. This one is not fertile." There was a black ring in the one that would be fertile – a wee black ring inside at the top of the egg. You could see it with the sun. I've done that myself too.

The generation of nowadays doesn't believe in things like that at all. They would laugh in your face. If I happen to say to my own family that my grandmother used to say that if you saw a certain thing, it was a bad sign, they laugh at me. They say, "Do you believe in that, mother?"

I think it's just that the generations are changing. Young children nowadays – they're bored. When they have their school holidays, they're bored. We were never bored. We had so much to do. We had so much to look forward to. Going down to the shore there with my grandmother in school holidays, that was really a holiday for me. Going to get those different things, and coming home and seeing things done with them. And we were always out helping. My grandmother, although she didn't have a croft, while she was able to, was always out helping – binding with different people, lifting potatoes. Everybody was the same in those days. They were out helping one another all the time.

We all talk Gaelic in the home. My sons were brought up in the Gaelic and it's Gaelic they talk all the time, and they prefer it to English.

When I was going to school, it was all Gaelic in the playground. You never heard an English word spoken. Children who were Gaelic speakers would be just kind of looked down on if they started speaking in English. But then, of course, incomers started coming in and that meant that when their children went to school, it wasn't so easy for the local children because they were hearing English in the playground and I think quite a lot of them were taken by it. I think they preferred to be speaking English, the same as the incomers were.

So, gradually, in the local community you would hardly hear any of the children speaking Gaelic. And now, in quite a lot of houses where there are children, I hear the mother and father speaking English to them instead of the Gaelic, and I don't believe in that at all.

But I think Gaelic is coming alive again. They're paying more attention to it in schools now and I think the children are getting more interested in it and starting to speak it. The younger ones are anyway. So it's good to hear them getting back into their native language.

I think Gaelic will survive.

Vice-Admiral Sir Roderick Macdonald, KBE

Ollach, Skye

I met Vice-Admiral Sir Roderick Macdonald in his home – a renovated and discreetly extended former black house – in the Braes area of Skye. He and his wife went to live there permanently when he retired at the end of his long and distinguished naval service. He spends his time pursuing a "second career" as an artist (he has exhibited in Naples, Edinburgh, and London), gardening, and playing an active role in community organisations.

I asked him what had attracted him to Skye.

I'm from a Highland family – my grandfather came from the Black Isle. I was born in Java. In those days there was very little Scots like my father could do for a career in Scotland and he spent the whole of his life in the Far East. He was involved in growing rubber, tea, and coffee in Java, Sumatra, the southern end of Borneo, and Malaysia. There were so many Scotsmen there that when they had an international golf match, it was Scotland v The Rest. The Rest included the Americans, the Dutch and the English.

I was only there until I was about five and a half because in those days there was some curious medical reason the doctors dreamt up which meant that children had to come home when they were five or six, otherwise something awful happened to them – they sprouted in the tropics or something. The Dutch children stayed. Nothing ever happened to them. But we were sent home at that age. Not for educational reasons; for medical reasons.

Ridiculous.

So I was sent to boarding school in Moffat and when I left that at 13, I went to Fettes in Edinburgh. And then from Fettes I passed the exam into the navy. That was just before the war. And I was in the navy for 40 years. So I'm Institutionalised Man. But I'm answering your question in a very circular way.

I was at Fettes and children then didn't go back and forward on visits – I didn't see my mother for three years at a time and I used to worry that I wouldn't recognise her when she came home – so I started having holidays with my grandmother in Glasgow. But it got very boring because there was nothing to do. So for a bit I worked on a farm at a place called Uplawmoor – which is somewhere near a place called *Baurheid* – as a wee boy in the holidays.

Then my father took me up to the Highlands, which I was very keen on, and I made friends with a crofter in Benderloch. His was a Gaelic-speaking family and I used to stay with them. I would camp outside and they fed me and everything like that in a house just like this, and the reason I don't speak Gaelic now is that they wouldn't speak it to me. Because I spoke English, they thought it was polite for them to speak English. So I never learned the language.

Then, after I joined the navy, I couldn't live up here in Scotland because the whole business of the navy was in the south – it's quite different now, the emphasis is in the north – but I used to spend my holidays as much as I could in the Highlands.

I looked for years for a croft house and when an old friend of mine was resigning from the navy and coming to live in Skye, I asked him to look out for one for me. The years passed and eventually I got a little letter about this house. I came up to see it and, after a lot of difficulties, I bought it – having taken the trouble to find out that no local wanted it. I didn't want to appear to be shoving somebody out. But I discovered that nobody would touch it with a barge-pole – no local anyway. They were quite wrong because they didn't realise how good these houses are. I mean, these will still be standing when all those modern jobs are rotted and blown down.

I don't know if I've answered your question very well. I suppose really that emotionally, and all the rest of it, I know that I'm a Highlander. I have always come back up here. In my last job in the navy I lived in Naples for nearly three years and the Italians couldn't understand why I'd go off when I had leave to some strange island called Skye, somewhere near the North Pole.

I've really put my roots down here. I feel part of the place. I don't regard myself as a total incomer, because I'm a Highlander and the Macdonalds were here much longer than many of the other clans.

I like living by the sea, I like the hills, and, oddly enough, I like this climate because it never ceases to change. It can be blowing like anything one minute and then the sun will come out. And you get these marvellous lights off the water so that you can barely look at it – it's like a burnished shield. It fires up into your eyes. It's a great place for a painter. The atmosphere is clear. And the sea isn't polluted yet, although people are trying like mad to change that – all the sewers go into the sea. Also, I like the people. And I'm mixed up with certain aspects of the culture of the Highlands because I play the pipes and I'm president of Skye Piping Society and Skye Highland Games.

I spent a lot of time in the navy learning how to deal with bureaucracy and that's a very minor contribution I can make to the community. I've always said that I don't want to get involved with politics or the council or anything like that, but if in any way I can help by handling something, by knowing who to write to, this is one of the things I feel I can do. I mean, I can't bake pancakes for the village fete, but I can probably write a letter.

In 1979 – I can remember the exact moment – I was walking my dog up near Duntulm Castle when I suddenly saw a huge thing which we call a VLCC. A Very Large Crude Carrier. These carry an enormous amount of oil – they're socking great things – and this one was coming southbound through the Minch and it all began ticking over in my mind.

I know what the Minch is like. It looks like a long strip of clear water of 12 or 15 miles, but it has got rocks sticking up right the way across and there are two holes through which ships can go. But these tankers have a turning circle of three-quarters of a mile and they take miles to stop. So if anyone made a mistake and the bottom of one of these huge things was ripped out, and it was full, going south, it would write off not just Skye and the Outer Hebrides, but the whole of the west coast of Scotland – and it would write it off for several years. It would destroy the wildlife – birds, scallops, fish. And no one would come to a B and B in a place that stinks of oil.

So I started writing to people about it – all the wrong people to start with. I wrote to a chap called Younger who was then Secretary of State for Scotland, and I got a reply back from a chap called Rifkind, who was his number two at the time, saying that it was nothing to do with him, and that I should contact the Ministry of Transport. So I wrote to them and I got a long thing back referring me to Highland Regional Council. So I went on and on and eventually I got pretty fed up, but I agitated and got various people interested and the next thing that happened was that they said, 'Oh very well, but we can't stop people going through there, we can only advise them not to' – because our Government is always very worried in case there is tit for tat somewhere else. But first the sea outside the Hebrides had to be surveyed because it hadn't been surveyed since the time of Captain Cook or something like that.

So that took about two years and then we had to go to the International Maritime Organisation because the tankers can be of any nationality and that took another few years to clear. But finally it was cleared and the charts now have a recommended route for tankers over a certain tonnage going round the outside – although it doesn't actually *prevent* them from going through the Minch.

I don't know how much the Minch is being used now because I don't live on that side of the island. But I think that on the whole most of them go round the outside. The northbound ones – the empties – can come through because although they could make a mess, it would be nothing like the mess a full one could make. The difficulty is that Government departments think that checking and monitoring is very expensive. It's not. You just ask the harbour masters at both ends which way the chap has gone, and although I believe most of them are behaving now, I'd like to know that it is one hundred per cent.

Jessie Macquarie

Salen, Mull

*Born and brought up on the home farm at Lagganulva in Ulva
Ferry on the west coast of Mull, Jessie Macquarie was employed
for years on Killiechronan Estate, mostly as farm manager.
Although she was only 53 when we met in April 1991, she was
able to do very little work. She had married Addie only seven
years previously. It was the lambing season and for the duration
he was having to live in a caravan in Quinish where they have 570
Cheviot ewes.*

We talked across her kitchen table in the village of Salen.

I've been in farming all my life but [holding out her swollen
hands] as you can see, I've got arthritis now. My hands are just
jiggered. The heart's willing but the flesh is weak, so I don't work
now.

When I first came down here to live, I was just bored to tears. I
didn't know what to do with myself. I was lost. I would go up to
the corner shop there and they would say, "Oh, here she comes
again. Bored to tears." I literally was, you know.

It was hard work, but it was very rewarding work. I mean, at
this time of year naturally you get dead lambs, but if you save a
lamb it's a fantastic reward to know that you did. Then you've got
your markings in a month's time. Then your shearing later on. I
used to compete at shearing competitions. I used to compete at
dog trials. I used to compete at ploughing competitions. I think I
was the only woman ever to compete at the ploughing matches.

•••

Photographs were produced of cups being presented, of treasured horses, prize-winning cattle, faithful dogs, and of a pig – Piggywig by name.

It was just the runt of the litter. I reared it on a baby's bottle. You know, it would come into the house and come to me and ask for its supper every night. It just ran about the yard at Killiechronan. In its young days I kept it in a tea box and it would run about the kitchen in the evening when we were in. And I would put it in the tea box with a hot bottle under its straw at night. You had to see it to believe it. Just a wee tiny thing. You could see all its ribs. But, by Jove, it grew into a big pig.

Aye, it broke my heart when it went away. And, you know, the night before it went to the slaughter house – we didn't eat it – it didn't come home for its supper. It used to go up and feed the hens with me and then it would caper about the green up there and it would come back down in its own time. That night it never came home. The next morning, I went up, shouting it, and it was in one of the sheds up the top buried in a heap of hay. And that made it all the sorer to put the poor blighter away to the slaughter house. That beast knew. I'm certain it did. That was the one and only night she never came home for her supper.

On a winter's night when we were kids, we spent the evening in the byre brushing cows and leading them on halters up and down the grip. How we were never killed I just don't know. When you stop and think back... And in those days all the cattle had horns.

Bedtime, you'd hear a shout at the house door, "It's time you were in," and you'd run in from the byre and go away to bed quite happy then. But they never worried about us. They knew fine we were out with the animals. But it was handy if you ever wanted to shift a cow somewhere. They were halter trained because we did it as kids.

I remember once we had twin calves and they were born at night after we were in bed. And the bull calf couldn't stand. His spine was weak and he couldn't stand. Father was just going to do away with him. My mother said, "No, leave it so the girls see him in the morning." And oh, we wouldn't let him kill that calf.

Well, we taught him to stand. We spent hours with him, putting a canvas stool under his tummy and working his legs for him – maybe one of us at his front legs, one at the back legs, and the other at the stool, moving the stool along. And, you know, that calf walked. He walked in a twist right enough; his tail was away round. And we had that beast until he was nearly two years old. Things like that you remember.

I think it would be drummed into us from an early age that tup lambs and bull calves are only here for a short time. You're fighting to bring lambs into the world but if you've got a tup lamb you know straight away it's for the market.

I was always keen on dogs. Very keen on dogs. We always had pups at home. Ach, I haven't run trials for quite a number of years now right enough. But I've got a young one there which I hope might do something.

They've got to have a bit of eye. And they've got to understand you – do as you tell them. None of this doing what they think sort of thing – although some of them do.

I've got an old bitch there. She's a good hill dog. I never ever ran her at trials because I somehow hadn't got the time just to train her. But see when you're working with ewes and lambs, she's just fantastic at gathering the hill. You just need to stand on a point and she'll go away out round the shore and round one knoll, and round the next, and she'll take everything off it. And a lot of folk have admired her for that – the distance she'll go out and bring in sheep. And she knows just where to go and look for them on the hill now.

It's just instinct. If it's in them, they're good. In fact, Addie did the lambing last year with a pup off her at seven months old. It was great at the lambing. He was tighter than my old bitch to catch a sheep. He would just come right in and just stare her in the eyes and the sheep is standing spellbound. You know? He's turned into a cracker of a dog altogether. He's just the softest big lump, yet the minute he sees a sheep, the nonsense goes completely out of his head. 'I'm at my work now and just leave me alone,' sort of thing.

•••

When you are walking on the hill there on your own, it's a marvellous feeling. You're hearing every sound of a bird or that. It's really very peaceful. I like the wildlife. You see rabbits, hares, deer, grouse, pheasants, all the other birds. Otters. It's not often you see them, right enough. You're quite lucky to see them. But I've seen them two or three times. The golden eagle of course; they're quite numerous about here too. As for the hoodie crow, they're far too numerous. They're our fox here. Desperate altogether. They're really bad. They'll take the tongue and the eyes out of a lamb in no time. I've seen them take the tongue out of lambs before they're born. That is true.

Summer was magic. Haymaking time was just fantastic. It was. To this day I love the smell of a newly cut field of hay. Beautiful.

I haven't heard the cuckoo this year yet. She's late. I think it's been too cold for her. Somebody said they've seen her, but that's bad luck to see her before you hear her. So they say anyway.

The first ploughing match I ever ploughed at was over in Quinish, and I think I got second that day. My brother was ploughing that day too but I beat him and some of the boys were saying, "Away home and show him how to plough," sort of thing. And then another year it was at Glenforsa out here and I won everything that year.

There are three different classes. There's the 10 inch, the eight inch, and then there's the 12 inch. And then there's the rig of the field – the best ploughed rig in that lot. I won that two years running and oh, the first year it was great glee, you know. Everybody thought it was great but when I did it the next year, some of them took it on the nose quite sorely. And I did it actually a third year although I wasn't awarded it. So I didn't go back to the ploughing match for years. It didn't bother me but it hurt my father because he was a champion ploughman all his days and he was really pleased that I had followed in his footsteps.

So then the ploughing match died away for a number of years, and then it was revived about 10, 12 years ago.

There was one fellow in particular always ploughed in the eight inch class and he would win it. Then, when it was revived, he came out in the 10 inch class and I beat him. And that made my day, just to beat that man.

Some go to an awful length for sorting the furrs – taking off a plough to put in the finish, and all the rest of it. I can't be bothered with all that carry on. If you can't set your plough so that the plough does it, you shouldn't be there at all. Anyway, he went in for the 10 inch when it started up again and I was in the 10 inch and some of the boys that were with him were saying I was too deep, I was too this, I was too that. I said, "Shut up. You go and plough yours and I'll plough mine." And, blow me, I got first. I beat him. I says, "Well, supposing I die tomorrow, I'll die happy. I beat you." I said it to his face. He didn't take it too bad. But some of his followers took it really bad.

You only got a wee bit to plough – maybe about the width of the kitchen here. You could do that in half an hour at normal ploughing, but some of them would take all day.

You had good fun. There was good crack and there was often a dance at night. We still have sheep dog trials and sheep shearing competitions. And a local show of course.

You'll not buy a potato that's cropped in Mull now, which is sad to say. There are very few do it. And you'll not get a house cow – a milk cow. Our milk comes from Nairn. That's something I miss since I left Killiechronan: our potatoes, our eggs, and our own milk. I really miss that.

I wouldn't change my life for anything. I've had no regrets about it. I think maybe it's my love for animals that has done that. That just about sums it up. My love for animals has been my life.

Lavinia Maclean-Bristol

Breachacha, Coll

Lavinia Maclean-Bristol, or the Honourable Mrs Maclean-Bristol to style her correctly, lives in Breachacha Castle on the south-east side of Coll with her husband. Throughout his army career Major Nicholas Maclean-Bristol had been determined that one day he would live on the island which was the home of his ancestors who were a branch of the Macleans of Coll.

In 1967, he founded Project Trust, an organisation which sends school-leavers abroad for a year to do voluntary work before going off to university. It started with three people going over to a slum school in Ethiopia. Twenty-four years later, 164 youngsters left for 16 countries. Before they went, each undertook a selection and training course at the Trust's headquarters in Ballyhaugh, Coll. Major Maclean-Bristol is the organisation's director. His wife is his assistant. The couple are English, and have three grown-up sons.

I first came here two months before we got married. Nick brought me for five days in February and showed me this ruined castle that his ancestors had created way back. I was only 19 at the time. It was so romantic – this old ruined castle and this handsome captain I was marrying. It was all too wonderful for words. But I never imagined at that stage that I would live here. Nobody has ever actually asked me, "Would you like to spend the rest of your days on Coll?" Never been asked that. [Laughter].

We came to live here in 1972. By this time Project was quite well established, and Nick decided to bring the organisation with him. Not only is he romantic, he's a historian and at the back of his mind was this idea that people from Coll had always gone out into the world. There had always been young men going out from Coll to seek their fortunes, or to join armies – there had been a lot of mercenaries from here in the past – and this had enriched the island because they came back with their new ideas and their wealth and kept the island alive. And Nick wanted to carry on that tradition of people going out into the world from Coll.

So we came here and we lived in this ruined castle with our small children. And we brought people here before we sent them abroad. Initially, they used to come along and help us with the development of the castle. They would dig holes and move boulders around and help with the reconstruction. But it was rapidly obvious that that wasn't a very good way of doing things at all because, with the best will in the world, they weren't very efficient. The ones that were there one week would undo all the good of the previous week.

The castle was pretty desperate when we moved in. It was extremely uncomfortable. There was no running water, there was no electricity, and there was no drainage of any sort. The walls hadn't been touched since 1750 and they were all crumbling. It was absolutely hotching with insect life. All sorts of horrible insects everywhere. You couldn't leave a sugar bowl out on the table at night without finding things in it in the morning. It had rats, and it had mice as well. It was incredibly cold and draughty because there was no heating at all. Washing nappies was just a nightmare because you couldn't get them dry. There was no washing machine – there was no electricity on the island *full stop*. All the water had to be carried in in buckets. All the dirty water had to be carried out in buckets. The chemical loo had to be emptied once a week or every three days, depending on how many people were there. We had no vehicle – we couldn't afford one – so we had to rely on the postman bringing things from the village.

I lived from week to week. Things were bound to get better. They might be better by the end of the week. I never thought about the next week, the week after, and the week after that. I've always been one to go sort of sniffing along the ground like a little animal, not looking from side to side. But I have a husband who has a great overview so I've always trusted him to look after the bigger things because I'm too busy looking after the minute detail from day to day – and that's how it works with the organisation itself.

So, if I look back at what I did, and what I put up with, it was incredibly daunting. But, from day to day, there was always a little ray of hope that things were going to get better: live for the day and perhaps it will improve.

At first, socially, it was very, very difficult. We were very cut off. People were very suspicious of us – the old guard were. I remember that one of the first things that happened to you when you arrived on the island was that you got roped onto the Mothers' Committee. I remember being faced with all these older ladies. Well, I thought they were terribly old. I suppose they were probably in their late thirties. And they used to glare at me if I was ever to suggest anything. I remember even voting against myself once, I was so scared. It was on some major issue like: should we bring in bought cakes for the Christmas party or should we make them ourselves? It was formidable. And they were very suspicious. They wouldn't include me in anything.

There was very little going on in those days – we're talking about 20 years ago. Things were much more traditionally Hebridean. There was a lot of ceilidhing in people's houses, but you weren't asked, and I came from a society where people would say, "Would you like to join in? Would you like to be part of our group?" Nobody asked. Nobody invited me. We were quite isolated in that way. We had lots of people staying – friends of ours who would come to help restore the castle, and volunteers, and people who'd come for a fortnight and stay for 18 months at one stage. Lots and lots of people in the castle, but we were outwith the main social life of the island.

But one of our neighbours had always been on our side and she was very influential within the community. She was very well thought of and what she said had quite an influence on the island.

She is our oldest ally – she and the man who drove the taxi, he'd done a lot with Nick before we married – and they were the two who really broke the ice. And gradually, gradually, gradually, people started to change.

We were the first of quite a number of families coming into the island. There'd been quite a dearth of incomers up till then. So we arrived, and then these other families arrived, and that was the beginning of change on the island. Young mothers came in who weren't prepared to do nothing but listen to what the old guard said. They weren't frightened of them. So we formed things and we expanded things. The Mothers' Committee up till then had merely had a Christmas Party once a year. We expanded it and fund-raised. We raised money for a playgroup. And, as soon as I got a bit of backing, I started to very, very gently suggest ideas. And people would come along who were prepared to put in an effort, to make things, and create things.

We started having picnics. All the old guard said, "Picnics? That's not what the Mothers' Committee is for."

We entertained the children. We changed the name of the committee to the Children's Entertainment Committee. The children's party changed. It's now a pantomime. There was all this pushing ideas through, always against the old guard who would say that we couldn't do this, we couldn't do that.

But, you see, this then had a counter effect. More groups grew up. There was a knitting group, and a men's club, and a whole lot of other things grew up. And the old guard got pushed aside. And the unfortunate thing is that a lot of the soul went out of the island as a result. For example, the committee would say, "Wouldn't it be wonderful to have a picnic? We'll have it on Sunday afternoon."

And at once you got the Free Church saying, "You can't have picnics on a Sunday afternoon."

And, for a while, we said, "OK, we can't have picnics on a Sunday afternoon."

But gradually things changed. Gradually, the old views were pushed out and with them, I think, went a lot of the Hebridean character because the Hebridean character was so much tied up with what the Free Church said and did. When I first arrived on the island, you never, ever went against what the Free Church said. But now, "who cares?" And once you lose the influence of the old guard and the Free Church, then you start to become just an island, not a Hebridean island. And I think that's what's happening here, and I suppose we were amongst the people who started changing things.

When I first came here, I felt very much alien to the culture. I really didn't understand it. And yet, funnily enough, when it disappeared and I was back in familiarity, in middle-England familiarity, I resented that really because I didn't like being associated with the English, with the incomers.

It was a fantastic environment for children. In the early days, because we weren't on the mainland, a lot of pressures were taken off them – pressures like what to wear to school, pressures to keep up with the Joneses. These didn't exist. We all swapped jeans. The biggest child on the island got the new jeans. We all got clothes at jumble sales. Now, it's different. It was much less affluent then. We were all much more of a muchness, when we all had young children. We started the playgroup from scratch and at one point we had 11 children in it – an enormous number of young children on an island this size. And that was a lot of fun because none of us had any money and we couldn't afford to buy toys, so we all made our own. And that was good for the children. It wasn't a materialistic society, that's the point I'm making. And the other point is that the pressures of security didn't exist. My middle son was the friendliest child out. He would talk to everyone and I was very pleased about this. My youngest one was rather shy and I'd say, "Don't be rude. You must talk to strangers. You must say hello to visitors."

Would you be doing that on the mainland? You would not. You would be doing exactly the opposite.

One of my expressions to my children when they were young

was "run free". They wanted to run across a meadow and not be able to be stopped. They had absolutely no road sense and would almost get themselves killed when we went to the mainland. They had the freedom to run across hills and do what they liked, when they liked. They'd go off for hours and hours, and it wouldn't worry me. They used to inhabit a world of their own. They would dig great earth works down in the dunes by the castle and play soldiers day in, day out. You couldn't do that in an urban environment.

So there was this freedom. It was an old-fashioned childhood. We didn't have television because we couldn't afford it, and, in any case, the picture was so appalling. But so what? They read. I suppose the way of life was 10, 15 years behind that on the mainland. It was old-fashioned, but not because I was consciously trying to bring them up like that. It was just that that was what the environment dictated. It was lovely for them.

Hugh MacLean

Barrapol, Tiree

Between the late 18th century and the post-First World War years, waves of islanders emigrated from the Hebrides to America, Canada and Australia. Some went voluntarily, with financial assistance. Others, in the darkest days of the Highland clearances, were rounded up like cattle and herded aboard waiting ships. For many, the truth lay somewhere in between.

Now, air travel and affluence make it possible for their descendants to return on holiday in search of their roots. Anyone of Tiree ancestry arriving there to look for information will inevitably be directed to Hugh MacLean's door.

Born in 1916, he lives with his wife, Sarah, on their croft.

I must admit, it was very little interest I had in genealogy when I was a teenager. But at that time, if a neighbour or a friend or an acquaintance visited you, that was the topic to be discussed – relations. I knew two or three elderly people that passed on long ago who were experts. Well, I have a retentive memory. So that's it. I still remember what I heard.

Going back to before the last war, people used to gather in neighbours' houses and have a game of cards or something like that. And then they'd have a smoke and a cup of tea or something, and then the stories started. The likes of me would be listening, you see. And I got a hold of all that, listening to the older ones. These boys were in their seventies and eighties at that time. They were very interesting and there were characters amongst them too. Very interesting characters. You'd get a laugh with them.

Everything is so serious now. You can't get a laugh at all. They haven't time for fun as the old ones had. The old ones were good to listen to and they always had a good quip. And a very sharp tongue to cut you off. Pleasantly. Nicely. I don't mean in a bad way. And, of course, your reaction would be: it's your day, but I'll get you yet. They wouldn't fall out about it.

Watching television and listening to the radio: these are the pastimes now. And television and radio have done away with all that and with other things. They have done away with musical talents too. When television and radio weren't there, people had to produce their own entertainment. When I was a boy, there were quite a few violinists on this island. There's not one now. There were more pipers on the island in those days too. Why? Because music is broadcast every day in life now. Mostly, it's modern music which, I admit, I *hate*. I've no time for it. I like the old stuff, the traditional stuff.

I am sorry to know that Gaelic is dying out here. That's the proper word. It's not just that I think it. I know it's happening. They're making an effort to preserve it. There are Gaelic teachers in the local school, but the tendency is that youngsters somehow or other prefer English. I don't know why.

An awful lot will be lost if the Gaelic culture dies. First of all, the music of the Celt. Oh yes... The Celtic music. The lilt of Scottish traditional music. There's nothing, to my ear, in the world like it. I have been used to hearing it all my life and my ear is tuned to it. You can get music from England, and from foreign lands too – and good stuff at that – but my ear doesn't understand it.

Take a good piper playing pibroch – the heavy traditional music of the bagpipes. To the person who doesn't know anything about it, it's a lot of squealing without any sense to it. But if you know the story that caused the composition of the tune, you can hear the pipe almost talking to you. That's how it is. You can almost hear what happened from the music of the pipe. There's something in it that just cannot be explained. That's how I feel. There's no doubt that modern music or foreign music is as good as any other, but for the Celtic ear it's the Celtic music that's wanted.

And another thing. You can never translate, say, a joke that was made up about something that happened in Gaelic. Supposing you translate it into English, it hasn't the same flavour at all. No, nor anything like it.

And the lovely Gaelic poetry. It would be terrible to lose that. We have had a lot of Gaelic poets on this island – good ones too. Fortunately, I have a lot of their works. Love songs. Tragedies. Praising the beauties of the island or the piece of land on which they lived. Elegies – some beautiful ones. All the islands had their own poets. Oh yes, some beautiful stuff.

I took a real interest in genealogy when I got to a mature age – in, say, my late forties. My uncle was an expert and he passed an awful lot of information to me. And I remembered what I had heard related by the older ones. I would have known a lot more if only I had listened better. The number of years I can go back depends on just who the people are and whether I've heard tell of their family.

They come here from all corners of the globe – in summer particularly, when they are having their holidays in this country. People who have roots in the islands like to come back and make inquiries. It started 10 or 15 years ago and it's getting busier and busier.

Some come from quite close by. A couple came here from West Loch Tarbert looking for information concerning their relations. They knew they were Campbells, but that was all I could get out of them. Now, that's not enough. There are many Campbell families on this island. But they dropped a clue eventually. The lady said, "My aunt told me that her father had a cousin, a seaman, a John Campbell, and he was lost when his ship foundered. I don't know when, but I know the ship's name."

"Yes? What was the ship's name?"

"The S.S. Opal."

"Good gracious. That's good enough for me," I said. "I know who you are now."

They need to give me a clue to give me a start. But sometimes they say that their great-grandfather was a MacKinnon, a MacLean, or a MacDonald, or whatever, and they know nothing else, so I'm stuck.

A year or two ago, a couple came here from New Jersey, USA. It was the lady who was looking for her ancestors. The gentleman was American-born. So, anyway, I could make nothing of it. She hadn't a clue, only that her grandfather was a sea captain and he was a MacKinnon. That was all. She couldn't give me any dates or anything else.

"That's not enough. I cannot trace you with that information."

And I almost gave it up. But, as a last resort, I said to her, "Tell me, do you know the names that were commonly used in your family? The male names."

She did, and my mind went back to Balemartine, to MacKinnons out in Balemartine there. But something wasn't fitting at all. Still, I kept them in mind although I didn't say anything.

"I don't know. I'm not sure yet. What about the females? What were the names commonly used for the daughters? Do you know?"

"Yes," she said. "I know some of the names, although I've never met these people."

She mentioned two or three. "But," she said, "There was one that had a very unusual name. Dona. Whether that's short for Donalda, I don't know."

"Well," I said, "We're coming close now. Do you know any of the married names of these women you mentioned?"

"Yes, one of them was married to a MacLean. And another was married to a Captain Shaw."

"That's it," I said, "I've got them now. That was Dona who was married to Captain Shaw. The best thing you can do now is to make straight back to Scarinish and meet Donald and Anne Kennedy. These are your blood relations – the nearest to you on

Tiree. And you may be lucky enough to meet a daughter of Mrs
Shaw. She's on holiday on the island at the moment."

As for my own people, they come across here occasionally.
They're over in Canada, from Manitoba right away out to
Vancouver. My grandfather was the only member of his mother's
family that remained in this country. There was Alan, John, Neil,
and Donald, that's four sons, and Mary and Anne, two daughters,
who went across there and never came back. Alan did come back
for a trip or two, but the rest never did. They went in the 1870s.
One of the sons was a seaman by profession and he had a coal
boat of his own and he was able to scrape together some sum of
money. He paid for the passage across and, of course, in those
days you'd get an assisted passage. There was a government grant
to get rid of the people.

Alan pegged out a farm for himself in Manitoba. In those days
all you had to do was peg out the ground you desired – mind you,
it was virgin prairie ground – and then negotiate the rent. He did
well with the farm but what made his money was the CPR. The
Canadian Pacific Railway was being built and it passed through
his farm. Well, that means compensation. He came back here two
or three times, but the others didn't. They had their mother with
them. Their father died before they left. I've got about 45 second
cousins I've never met out in Canada.

I can go back some bit in my own family alright. There are
more Hugh MacLeans in Tiree than me. But if you were to
describe me in Gaelic, you would put it this way: Hugh, son of
Donald, son of Hugh, son of Hector, son of Alan, son of John.
That's me. That's how we work it out.

Morag Munro

Borve, Harris

Born in 1948 in Collam in the Bays area of Harris, Morag Munro lives in Borve with her husband John and their children Roddy Angus and Donna. As organising secretary for Harris Council of Social Service, she has one of several offices housed in a former hostel for Tarbert's Sir E. Scott School.

At the time of this interview, the island's children could only study up to Standard Grade level in the school. If they wanted to continue with their education they had to board in Stornoway to do a fifth and sixth year at the Nicolson Institute. This set-up was not ideal, but at least it was an improvement on Morag's day...

Pupils intending to take Highers had to leave Harris at the end of second year – and it wasn't to go to Stornoway in those days because Lewis was in Ross and Cromarty and Harris was in Inverness-shire. So we had to go to Inverness or Portree, although in my year Portree wasn't an option because there were no hostel places there. So it had to be Inverness. It made very little difference whether you went to Portree or Inverness – they were both across the water and that meant being away all term. You went away in August and came home at Christmas-time and again at the Easter break, and then in summer.

I think we were quite resilient about it. There were some who gave up, but they were few. In fact, there were some – from south Harris for instance – who left home to go away after primary school. They went straight to Inverness to do their first year. One or two of those had to give it up. They were just too young to be away from home so they came to Tarbert and went away again at the end of second year.

I think maybe the attitude to education is changing now, but when I was in school there was no question of me saying, "I don't want to go to Inverness. I don't want to continue with my education. I want to leave school at 15." That option just never occurred. If you were capable of carrying on, you did. It was still a kind of privilege then. A lot of us were children of parents who had ability but because of their families' financial situation they couldn't carry on with their education.

My own father for instance was very able but his mother was a widow with five children and she refused to let him go away. It was just impossible. She couldn't afford it. In those days you had to pay for board and lodgings. The welfare state was not in place.

So I think my generation were sons and daughters of people like that, people who felt we were having a privilege that they didn't have. And we were very conscious of that. I didn't even feel that the option of not doing well was open to me. There was no way I was going to fail my exams. I worked and made sure I didn't.

I enjoyed my fifth and sixth years but I don't think I enjoyed my third and fourth. Going away was something you had to do and you accepted that. You had the opportunity and you had to take it. I didn't look at it that way then; it just didn't occur to me that there was an alternative. I didn't feel resentful or anything. I didn't feel forced into it. It was just an attitude that this was the right thing to do. Your parents said to you, "Look, you have the opportunity to become educated, have a good job. You'll have an easier life compared with what we had." So I think you were resigned to the difficult parts of it like being homesick, being away from home at 13 or 14.

One thing it did for us was to make us independent. We fairly stood on our own feet. We were forced to. You didn't depend on your parents because they weren't there. Your contact with them was by writing once a week. So if you had a problem, you had to work it out.

I think we were very naive. We were immature in comparison to our counterparts. Town life was very different from what we knew. Going back to Inverness now, I see that it's a very nice place and the people seem very nice – and it might be that we put up a barrier ourselves – but at that point we felt that Inverness people were cold and unfriendly. That's the way we saw them at the time. They used to call us "teuchters" and take the Micky out of us quite a bit about our accent and our general ignorance. So we stuck together and became more "teuchter" than ever. I'm not talking about the Harris people who lived there. In fact, some of them used to take us out for weekends and meals. There was one particular lady that we went to every week. She used to give us a lovely big spread and a whole crowd of us would unashamedly go to her house.

After moving to Glasgow to take a diploma in business studies and a teacher training course, Morag returned to the islands to take up posts in the Nicolson Institute and the Sir E. Scott School. She remembers her student days as being happier than those in Inverness...

That might have been because I was older, or because I thought that the people were friendlier. I don't know.

Of course, I had relations in Glasgow. For the first year, I lived with an uncle and mixed with an older cousin who kept an eye on me. I think my mother was quite relieved about that. If my son or daughter was going away, I'd be a lot happier if there was somebody they could go to who would keep an eye on them – somebody they could go to when they ran out of money and couldn't afford to buy their tea. That kind of support was always very useful when you were an impoverished student. I'm sure that people knew why you were suddenly turning up on their doorstep at a certain time in the evening.

I'm not looking forward to my children going away. Once that happens, never again do you have the kind of family unit you have when the children are small and everyone is at home at a certain hour every evening and in bed at night. But maybe it's not that different here from other places. No matter where you are, children reach a stage when they want to leave home.

I think to some extent this is one of the best places to bring up a family. Somebody said the other day that it's the last outpost of civilisation. We are reasonably well protected as yet from a lot of the problems that children come up against in other areas.

Drugs haven't penetrated – in Harris at least – for instance. I don't know whether they have come to Lewis or not, but glue sniffing has certainly reached Stornoway. As far as I know, that hasn't penetrated here – although obviously it might have done and we may be ignorant of it.

The other thing is that although moral standards are being eroded here as in every other place, it is happening more slowly. Maybe that's got something to do with the fact that it is a small place, a close-knit community. We live in an area which has respect for biblical standards. Petty crime is really very scarce. And certainly there is a general disapproval which provides restraints. Although, as I say, it is changing even here.

Something else I like about staying in Harris is the open space – the freedom children have compared to those in the town. We go away on holiday every year to Glasgow or East Kilbride or one of the cities, and the children love it and so do I. We enjoy the shops and all the things we miss at home. But as far as day to day living is concerned, I think children here are very fortunate. I can let mine out and they can roam the hills and have very healthy pastimes because of the great outdoors.

Our costs are higher here. That is a big disadvantage we face. In general terms the economic problems we have are because of higher costs. It is very difficult for us to attract a major industry to the island because its overheads would go sky-high. We are isolated so things are more expensive. On the other hand, there are some things that counteract that. For instance, it is a crofting community and people have sheep so they can save on meat. There is peat available so they can cut that and save on fuel costs. They can grow potatoes. That all helps to eke out the income, although obviously people like old age pensioners are probably worse off because they are too old to work a croft or cut peat so they can't take advantage of these economies in the way that others can.

But any economic disadvantages faced by islanders today pale when compared with the hardships endured by previous generations.

The struggles of the past do affect us and they rear up still. On the subject of landlords for example, you still find people being wary if an estate changes hands. The past affects the attitude to salmon poaching. That kind of thing.

In the old days, the landlords and their sporting parties would fish the salmon out of the rivers for sport and live it up in the big house while the people who lived round about were very short of food. The people believed that the fish – particularly the salmon – did not belong to any single person. They were God's provision for everyone. They came from the sea into the rivers and it was never really accepted very much in those days that it was right for the landlord to have access to them purely for sporting reasons while people round about lived on next to nothing. The islanders didn't have any access to the provision that was there on their doorstep. And I think that has affected the attitude of people today to the likes of poaching. I think in general they don't think it is a crime.

Of course, poaching has changed. In the past, people went to the rivers and fished a fish because their families were hungry. Now, you do have people who do it for commercial gain, which is a different thing altogether. But for the general person who went and poached a salmon for the good of his family, it was never considered to be a crime and I think the attitude to that has lived on.

Dr. John A. J. Macleod, DL

Lochmaddy, North Uist

Like his parents before him, John Macleod is a doctor. He was brought up in Lochmaddy where his father, a Lewisman, was the local GP. John followed him into the practice after spending the early part of his career in hospitals in Glasgow and London.

His interest in North Uist extends far beyond providing its people with general health care. He has conducted studies on the island diet, and blood pressure levels; he has campaigned to persuade fishermen to wear flotation vests, and to have the local licensing board use observers to ensure that alcohol is not sold to people who are already drunk; and has raised the ideas of job-sharing subsidies for crofters, and a co-operative which would make feasible the marketing of locally grown vegetables. He is also a Deputy Lieutenant of the Western Isles. He is married to Lorna, and has two sons and a daughter.

Why did he choose to return to North Uist?

I saw what was happening with patients in practices immediately round the hospitals where I was working on the mainland. They were either coming in themselves, or there seemed to be a very great tendency on the part of their doctors to over use the hospital. That is one of the unfortunate things about being a junior doctor in a hospital – you tend to get to know more about the practitioners who are not awfully good rather than the ones who are good, because the good ones are looking after their patients more so you don't see them to the same extent.

If you're a certain number of miles from a hospital, it means you have to think more and it keeps you and the patient together more on things. I think even if I'd settled on the mainland, I'd have tended to be 25 or 30 miles from a hospital.

So, over the years, I had felt that I would like to do general practice at a distance from a hospital, although I wasn't very happy about being in a single-handed environment. But, just at that time, the doctor in Benbecula was taking on a partner and he felt that he'd be able to offer me occasional afternoon and evening cover. That made it easier. So I came back here in partnership with my father in 1973, and he retired in October 1974.

Island life is more a man's life. The girls bail out on the whole and this is a problem within the islands. I think you'll find that women do that in remote areas on the mainland too – they tend to move in to where the shops and facilities are. Here, it is very much a man's world – it's an outdoor world. Most people have got ground of some sort – that's why they're here.

I'm particularly aware of a gross excess of bachelors here because I've measured it. I think it's got grave implications for the long-term future of the island if you want to keep Uist stock going. There is a huge shortage of women between the age of 17 and 40 on the island. It's not so obvious down in South Uist, I don't think – but I haven't measured it there.

It's the sort of thing that can be lost in population studies. Official statistics may not show it because for the Western Isles as a whole, it's not very obvious. That's probably because there's such a mass of girls living and working in Stornoway. The numbers there are so great that they could obscure the figures elsewhere. But down here, it's obvious, and it affects how the men behave because no matter what men say, young women in the company are a stabilising influence. So there's a tendency to get boozed excessively at times [although, he says, he doesn't know that alcohol abuse is any more of a problem on the islands than it is anywhere else] and to say, "Why the hell will I bother going to the dance? I'll just go and have a dram." And then, "Why do I bother going to the pub? I'll just stay at home." This can happen, and I think you'll find that that applies to quite a number of other isolated communities.

A bit of bad news I've got for you is that the MacDonalds are dying out. They're dying out quite rapidly. The MacLeans are increasing – they seem to be continuing to have quite a number of children – but the MacDonalds have an awful lot of bachelors. And MacDonald was so much a North Uist name. Our notes in the surgery are shifting. There's a big increase in the names before M, which tend to be mainland or English names – As, Bs, Ds, and Hs.

In the Seventies, there were complete families of North Uist stock coming back to the island to live. That has stopped, and it seems to be that the people coming now are couples in their fifties and sixties who have no connection with the island and who have not got their children with them – couples whose families may not develop any particular affection for the island. Some come because they're involved with the military, some just come because they've been here on their holidays at some time.

It's very difficult to tell what sort of effect this has had because there have been so many changes with electricity coming, the causeway being built between here and Benbecula, the car ferries, increased travel, television, but I would think that the people coming in are having very little detrimental effect compared with, for example, Mull in the 1950s, which we hear talked about a lot. Being this bit further out from the mainland, anyone coming here is probably going to have something they feel they can do. I do suggest this also to North Uist people who are thinking of retiring back to the island: they should come at a time when they can contribute their own thing, and can establish themselves in their own right rather than as somebody's cousin. When you go back home for a fortnight in the summer, you're just loaded with invitations. But if you retire and you come back to live on an island, the invitations happen once. Your cousins have you once, and that's about it. You've then got to establish yourself with people who are not your cousins. So it may be better for people who are retiring to stay where they are on the mainland, and come back on extended breaks instead.

More of the young are staying on in the island than there were 20 years ago, because there are more facilities for them. Mains electricity only came here in 1965/66. Until then there was no capability for a proper garage apprenticeship. There was no job for an electrician. Nothing connected with electricity. So there has been a gradual increase in that sort of thing, and the army are doing a fantastic job offering apprenticeships, and these young chaps tend to stay on afterwards or they go to work for one of the local companies.

But, really, I think the employment thing has to be looked at. Something that I have brought up in the past is that the Government talk about this or that small building being turned into a factory, and because it employs 10 men, they say it's supporting 10 families. Now, that's not true a lot of the time. You've got to look and see if those people are married or not, or if they're at the stage where they're going to get married and have children. These claims have to be looked at and challenged.

It's possible that somebody should come in and look at things in a different way – look at what sort of employment we need here. It might be that what is needed is an all-female employment unit with different grades of employment in it. The example I sometimes quote is that of a marine biology lab where you could have your honours graduate as a director, then technicians, down through someone who is just a technical assistant, to a cleaner. That might be what the island needs rather than something that is going to employ 10 men. Somebody has got to look at it from a different point of view and not just listen to the demands and pressures from vociferous people.

Another suggestion I've made is that there should be a subsidy for job-share for crofters because the land has deteriorated. That is true throughout the islands – and one of the reasons is that there's not so many cattle now, or even if the total is the same, they're concentrated into one or two hands, whereas it used to be that everybody had a cow or two. People have gone over to sheep. You can't manage cattle if you're in a nine to five job because you need daylight hours for tending to them, but you can manage sheep. At the moment the crofter has got to have a full-time job to support his family. So he can scatter fertiliser on a field to make hay for his sheep, and that's it. He can't go out in January to drain, he can't go out in February to take seaweed up from the shore. He hasn't got the daylight hours. But give him job-share, and he does. What's needed is a subsidy to cover the employer's extra tax and National Insurance contributions and to cover the individual's National Insurance contributions. If that was done, it would let the crofter go back to cattle, or go over to goats, or some other animal that people may decide is going to be good here. Or he could have turkeys, or chickens, or something of that sort. It would get him away from sheep and the ground would benefit from that. The land would be brought back up again and the place would become far more productive. So that's another hobby horse I have.

I'm worried just now by some of the things I've noticed about the population change. I think that there is good stock – good breeding stock, good character – in the North Uist people and that it's in danger of vanishing.

People will talk about the North Uist people as being middle-of-the-road – very reliable. They don't have the ups and downs that you get further north where the pendulum swings very greatly, not just in communities, but in an individual's life.

But although the population is going through a change, there are certain things that will continue through certain lines – customs and ways of doing things and saying things will continue in particular families always. If you were here at the cattle show or the games, I could point people out to you in a crowd and even as you went towards them to meet them, you would realise that you were going to meet somebody special. You would see that man, and his shoulders would go back just that much, and he'd look at you in a different way. It's a subtle little thing, but it's there. And that sort of thing will continue right through particular families.

There's a lovely illustration of the island character, which I only came across by chance. A friend of mine was travelling on a ship and in that ship he found a cruising club magazine and he copied out a passage and sent it to me. It was a letter from somebody from Glasgow who had been cruising and he landed at Barra or Vatersay. He went up and the local person he met was polite and nice to him and the man from the yacht said, "Could we have some eggs, please?"

And the man said, "But I haven't got eggs."

"But you've got hens."

"Oh well, that might be, but it doesn't mean that I've got eggs for sale."

And the conversation deteriorated and the local man had started off so polite and it ended up with him referring to "you and that woman that's with you," rather than "you and your fine wife," which was the way it had started.

So there is this very shrewd, very capable, very reliable, stock of people through many of the islands, but on this island perhaps they've stayed on more. They're very, very good and that streak will continue, but you've got to be in amongst the people to see it because they won't be the ones who'll come forward.

David Howitt

Glenforsa, Mull

David Howitt is a busy man. He is a photographer, he writes books, he does forestry work, he runs the Mull airfield, he designs and builds his own radio controlled aeroplanes, he hires out cars, and he and his wife Pauline have a craft shop strategically placed above the pier in Craignure.

A friendly character, he plied me with books of local interest and postcards, and suggested names of people I should meet. We talked – he so rapidly that I was thankful I was using a tape recorder and not shorthand – in the shop.

Born in 1940, he came to Mull in 1959 when his family moved from North London to take over a hotel. As an incomer, and as someone who has witnessed the massive increase in the number of people settling on Mull, he seemed the right person to talk to about how outsiders take to island life.

I've seen 'em come and I've seen 'em go. A lot of people just spend a very short time here. Maybe a year or two years. They see the island with a lovely sunset in May or June, before the midges, or before the long wet monsoon period starts, and they've got this idealised image. Mind you, if you live in London almost anywhere is going to be paradise compared with there. A lot of them come from the home counties. They are very largely English. A lot of northern English as well.

We don't resent them. My wife is English for a start, so I'd better not! But they have got rather a brash way of handling things.

Let's face it. I'm an incomer myself. I've only been here for 30-odd years. I'm very much an incomer as far as the old locals are concerned.

There are quite powerful pressure groups. And, you know, there are some long-haired hippies. As a dear old friend used to say, "The last one off the boat is the leader." You'll find there are these people who have been here a couple of years and they start chucking their weight around and get themselves elected onto this committee and that. I look upon them as the unwashed – you know, people from the south with a sociological degree or something like that. Usually single parents with a couple of kids. These are the ones you see causing a stir. I'm being specific about a small element.

In the late '60s, early '70s, there was a very nasty hippie element here with drugs. Very much so. They were rooted out. The local bobbies and, I think, the local people got together. They would tip the police off and they would make raids with tracker dogs to sniff up the stuff.

They got rid of them. Fortunately, that's gone. They're no longer here.

In the main, incomers integrate very well.

The people, I would say, who don't integrate are, shall we say, the incomers with a lot of money who live in the isolated communities around the island and they mix with their own type. Mull used to be called the "Officers' Mess." It was very much the English upper class. And there is still quite an active sort of coterie. There are quite a few of these people around and people try to break into it. At the apex, of course, is Lady Maclean at Duart Castle. "Oh, we were invited to Duart Castle" – this is the ultimate in the Mull social scene.

But in the main, the gentry are very well liked here. Lady Maclean is a real character. And Lord Maclean. He was a great old pal of mine. You ask anybody on the island: he was well liked. And she's well liked as well.

He organised *the* wedding. Charles' and Diana's.

•••

The island has changed in the last 30-odd years – changed quite significantly. Fast-growing conifers, fish farms, a tremendous influx of people.

In the year before the ferry started here [at Craignure] in the 1960s, there were a few hundred cars brought to the island. The year after, when the ferry actually started here, thousands of cars came across. It opened the whole place.

The incomers have brought wealth. There's no question about it. And brains. A lot of people who settle on the island have got qualifications. They've got a degree or they've been business folk, and they apply that education and that previous experience either to making money or to doing up a house, or to integrating as best they can in the society up here.

You could say the influx has had a deleterious effect, that the English have swamped the Gaelic culture. But I wouldn't say that. There is very little here for the indigenous Gael to live and work on Mull. There are only a finite number of shepherds. And the Forestry Commission... There were over 100 people employed by the forestry at one time. Now, it's all chiefs and no indians. They are all executives and very few of the executives, the chiefs, are actually from the island. They've all got their own vehicles... And when you see the topographical changes they've wrought on Mull in the last 30, 40 years... It seems astonishing that only about 30 people are employed on Mull by the Forestry Commission now. From the employment point of view it just doesn't hold a candle to even fish farming.

I've got three Scottish grandparents. The weak link in the whole lot is my father. He is English. Even he's not all that bad: he's a Cumbrian. During the war he was building aerodromes and after the war there was this tremendous re-building programme and he was around houses and factories all over England. I was at 12 different schools. I was at school in Wales, down in Hampshire, Birmingham, Darlington, all over the place.

I came up to Scotland in 1958 when my grandfather died and that is the first I can remember of Scotland as such. Within a year and a half I was up here permanently. That was it. I can remember going to his funeral in Edinburgh and despite the horror of the occasion, it just seemed to me to be home.

We bought a country house here which had been run as a hotel in 1959. It had been the old sort of manor house of the estate... Well, in fact, it was a sort of shooting lodge for one of the old toffs way back in the 1870s, 1880s. I was there for about a couple of years and then I went off to university and I became a teacher. I went to Ayr Academy and I taught there until the raising of the school leaving age and comprehensive education. The final straw was comprehensive education. Kids had been coming along who were highly motivated, nice, nicely dressed – the worst punishment you could give them was to ban them from playing for the First XV at rugger for a fortnight. And when it went comprehensive, the whole ethos of the school went down. The pupils couldn't have cared less. I was quite pleased to get out of teaching.

In 1971, I came back. Pauline and I got married in '73 and we've been here ever since. To tell you the truth, I get homesick when I go to Oban now – I miss Mull. I really, genuinely do. We don't go abroad. Glasgow is a big thing for us now. You really become very insular. Well, I've become very insular. I feel uneasy when I'm away from Mull. When I first came here I said, "Right, I'm going to give it a six-month trial." Six months. And I'm still here and have no desire to leave. None whatsoever.

I'm not a Gaelic speaker although I'm very, very interested in Gaelic and I'm very anxious for my daughter to learn it.

The people are very difficult to draw out. Let me give you an example of that. There was an old boy, old Donald, who came from Burg in the north of the island, and there was a dear old lady, old Chrissie Burgh who was from Burgh [in the south-west], and they were both fluent Gaelic speakers. That was their first language. About three years ago, I offered to take Donald down to meet her. I said I would take him down, I had a job to do down there, and would he like to come and meet this dear old lady that he had never met before?

"Oh no, I don't think that would be very proper."

And they never did meet. And they had this common language. They could have talked.

It's definitely a dying culture. Although they're resurrecting the Gaelic language *per se,* it's not the same. It's very much Runrig and the modern thing. The old traditions are going.

There are a good few Gaelic speakers on the island and the trouble is you've got this gulf between you. If you're not a native speaker, there's no point in even learning it because you can't really get their meaning. There's such a gulf. But this culture is always there. Hidden, just around the corner, is this subterranean thing – this lovely Gaelic culture. For me, it's a very attractive thing.

Kenny Campbell

Vatisker, Lewis

Born in Vatisker in 1910, Kenny Campbell attended the local school before winning a bursary for the Nicolson Institute in Stornoway. His career followed a familiar Lewis pattern: fishing, sailing the world's oceans (suffering a severe leg injury in the mid-Atlantic rescue of survivors from a sinking ship), and weaving Harris tweed in a shed outside his house.

He never married and lives alone in the family home. When we met, he reflected on the past and – in a tone which was curious rather than critical – the attitudes of Lewis's younger generation.

Should I refer to him as Kenny or Kenneth?

I had another brother called Kenneth. There were two of us, you see, with the same name. We were called after different Kenneths. So they called me Kenny to distinguish between us. In my day there were large families and they called you after relatives. Most of the names here nowadays are not Scottish. Especially the girls – "Yvonne" and whatnot. What's wrong with the good old Scottish names? Why would anybody call their children by foreign names, I can't understand.

The young people now don't speak Gaelic. Although they have it, they don't speak it. I don't know what's wrong with them. If you speak to them, they'll answer you in English. That's happened since 20 years ago. If it keeps like that, the next generation won't have any at all.

I think it's daft if they have a language of their own to lose it like that. I think anybody is better with two languages than with one. On the Continent there – in Holland, Belgium, Germany – nearly everyone is bilingual. Some of them are trilingual. But here, once they've heard English, they want to forget everything else. And the English language is a commercial language. There's no beauty in it compared with Gaelic. That's my opinion anyway.

Look at the songs and the poetry that were composed in Gaelic. It's a more poetic language and a more friendly language. It doesn't matter where in the world you go, if anybody is talking Gaelic, you strike up an acquaintance with them right away and they strike it up with you as soon as they hear you have it.

My grandfather was lost on a fishing boat. The boat overturned and there were six of them in it. Another boat picked up three of them. Three of them were lost and my grandfather was one of those lost.

The widow of another lived in that house over there with a son and a daughter. They were young and her husband was lost on that boat. Well, the young fellow, he was only a baby. I don't know if he was even born when his father was lost. But there was an uncle who was a minister across in Canada and when the boy grew to be 17, he went across to Canada and he worked himself through university there.

He only died two or three months ago. He was 99.

His daughter was here last year and I was speaking to her. She was about 60 then – a district nurse in Vancouver – and she was telling me her father was in an old people's home and he used to wander in his mind and she said that when he was like that, nobody could understand what he was talking about because he was talking Gaelic all the time. He'd been away for 80 years and as soon as he lost his memory, the Gaelic came back.

The young people nowadays, if they go away for a fortnight they're not speaking it when they come back.

Hebridean emigration was nothing new when that fatherless young man crossed the Atlantic in the first decade of this century.

Generations had preceded him. And another generation was to follow.

In his book, Metagama – A Journey from Lewis to the New World, Jim Wilkie notes that around 800 of the island's young chose to emigrate to Canada in a 12-month period during 1923-24.

Lewis was grief stricken at the end of the First World War. Out of a total population of 29,600, 1,151 servicemen had died. The devastating blow of the Iolaire disaster [see page 98] immediately followed. Little wonder therefore that, encouraged by state assistance with the fare and the prospect of employment and an improved standard of living, so many young people were enticed away to a new life in a new country in the 1920s. Kenny Campbell remembers this wave of emigration well...

That was just before my time. When I came to earn, that was the time the depression was starting in America. People stopped going there. A lot of them came home.

There was nothing for you here after the First World War. You see, before the First World War the fishing was the main thing. Herring fishing. But after the war there was no outlook for the fishing. That's when they emigrated. The Canadian Government used to send people here to urge people to go over to settle in Canada.

I was going to school then but I knew those that went from around here. There were three ships went. 1923 was the Metagama, and 1924 was the Marloch and the Canada.

After these people went the place was lonely. The young people were all gone.

Do you know how many people were lost in this street during the Great War? There are only 17 houses. I think there were 11 people lost in 17 houses. That was a terrible loss for a small village like this. All over Lewis was like that. There were quite a few lost from this village in the Second World War too. About half a dozen. My own brother was lost in the Second War. He got married the winter before it started.

My father was in the Navy in the First World War. Of course, I don't remember much about that. I was only from four to eight years. But I remember the Iolaire disaster as well as anything. We heard about it in the morning – the morning after.

There were a lot of people coming home the night it happened. There were no cars then. People went to meet them in gigs. Well, when they came home in the morning they woke people up and told them the boat had gone down. They didn't know who was saved. Through the day they got word.

My father came home from the war the next night again. He had two cousins – two brothers – who were both lost on the Iolaire. I can remember well. My father and two others were walking to Stornoway every day for three or four days, looking at the bodies as they came ashore to identify them. They identified one of the brothers but the other one never came ashore. They never got his body at all.

We built this house in 1930. It was a black house we had until then. A few of the black houses were about until after the Second World War. The people in them were too old to start building new houses, but they died out and there's no such thing as a thatched house around here now. It was a good thing that these houses went away. They were very warm and friendly and that, but everybody wants to live in comfort.

Every croft here was tilled right up to the door in my own young days. Potatoes and oats and barley, these were the main things; some vegetables, etcetera.

We only had a small croft compared with others here. About three acres. But every inch of it was tilled. The first time we got an enlargement was when my uncle died. He had no family and he left us his croft. That was another four acres. After that, a few years ago, a cousin died and she left us her croft too.

The boys were always at the shore in my day. I think the sea was bred in them some way or other. They were always down there watching the boats go out. That was in the old days of sail. It was a great sight to see the boats going out and which was the faster one. [Laughter].

Every village had a ceilidh house. People used to gather – the old people and the young people too. You heard all the old stories about the history of the place: the people who lived here, the people who left for Canada or Australia, what they did over there, the people who stayed. There was a lot of talking about the fishing and the seamanship – the wild days they were out at sea, and what happened. A lot of people were lost here from boats.

All that was handed down from generation to generation – the stories of these people. When you heard the story of your own people, it affected you. You knew they were men and that was that. And good men. They were good men at sea and on shore.

I don't think young people nowadays have got any conception of history at all. They don't care about it. We learned from the ones before us the things that happened. We knew the history of the place, the history of the people. But when you ask young people nowadays, they don't know a thing.

Anonymous

The following took place in the home of the person referred to here as A. I asked him for an interview because I had been told that he has "second sight". Stories of such a phenomenon abound in the Hebrides. Many a fascinating evening can be spent round the fire listening to them, although you need a good nerve when it comes time to step out into the darkness to go home.

A agreed, with a little reluctance, to talk to me. However, he insisted on remaining anonymous out of fear of being "pestered with folk". B happened to be visiting him at the time. To obviate speculation about identity the island is also nameless.

A: Second sight is a premonition of a death that's going to occur. I first got these premonitions when I was three years of age. It started when I was in my uncle's house. That's one thing I never forgot. I heard this hammering going on upstairs and I remember that I started crying. No one else could hear it and my uncle got on to me, but my father said, "You better leave the boy alone because you never know, he may have something that we're not aware of."

A few years later when my grandfather died in the same house, they had to use hammers to break open the chest where the shroud was. They kept shrouds in the houses at that time, and they had to break open the chest because they couldn't find the key. When I heard the hammering, I told them that that was what I had heard before.

At the age of three, I was too young for them to explain to me what it was. I wasn't aware of having second sight until I was well up in years – nine or 10, or something like that. That was when I discovered what was transpiring.

Sometimes you don't know that it's actually a premonition. If you were seeing someone, you would think that it was a living being you were looking at. You might think that you had actually seen the person until somebody would say to you, "That's impossible, he wasn't in the village last night." Or, "You couldn't have seen him last night, he was with me all evening."

There's nothing to be frightened of. It's something like an inward eye. It's not really in your vision at all. You could have better eyesight than I have, but you still wouldn't see what I was seeing. Although, it appears that you can pass your vision to somebody else if you're touching them. That has happened to my wife.

It can be a smell. When I was young I could smell death when I walked through the door of a house. I could smell it straight away. I'd feel sick until I came back out. Many's the house I went into and had difficulty in controlling myself.

I've never seen anybody that was very close to me. I don't know why that was kept off me. I've never seen anything that would upset me. It was usually neighbours and distant relatives and so forth. That's how I was anyway. I don't know how others are.

One thing that is quite a mystery is that anything you see, you go on seeing it until you actually understand what it is and who it is. It keeps repeating itself until you get a full picture. Once you recognise the person involved, you never see it again. That's the way it was with me. I would keep on seeing a figure until I recognised who it was.

B: My mother had an uncle – my mother told me this story – and he used to go away ceilidhing at nights and he told my grandmother that he was seeing a man beside him every night he went out. He couldn't figure out who it was. But one morning, he told my grandmother that he had seen this man again the night before and he told her, "I took my bunnet off, and he took his off too." That was when he realised that it was himself. He was dead within a year. He hadn't recognised himself until he had taken his bunnet off and the person walking beside him did the same.

A: If an image wants to be recognised by you, you can see it anywhere. I've seen one or two prowling around here when the person involved was away off the island altogether at the time.

You would never talk to anything like that. Well, I never spoke to anything like that anyway, so I wouldn't know what would happen if I did. In my younger days, I used to hear that anyone who was gifted with second sight should never be the first to speak to anyone at night. You were warned about this. My father warned me. If you were gifted like this, you should always let the other person talk to you first.

And you wouldn't disclose to anyone what you had seen, because you were only going to upset somebody. But many's the time I let the cat out of the bag, as the saying goes.

I remember one instance when I was employed on the mainland and I happened to be at home on holiday. That was in 1958. I brought a motorcycle home with me because I was building a house on the island at the time and it was handy for going back and forward. On this occasion I went to my brother's house to collect some joinery tools and at the end of the day's work I went to return the tools and I continued on my way home. When I turned left at the church there, I noticed this woman walking by the roadside ahead of me. I recognised her there and then as being a Mrs Kennedy. When I was passing her, I noticed that she looked very pale but I thought nothing of it at the time since she was well up in years.

Anyway, the following day, I headed back to the house I was building and when I got there a neighbour called me over for a cup of tea. We chatted away about different subjects, and I happened to mention that I had passed Mrs Kennedy on the road the previous evening and that she didn't look very well. On hearing this, all the folk present looked at one another and one of them said that Mrs Kennedy was confined to bed, and had been for weeks on end. That was when I noticed that I had put my foot in it. I tried to explain that I must have made some sort of mistake. But they knew me too well and they knew that I had seen something right enough. Mrs Kennedy only lived a couple of weeks after that.

I can remember going through two funerals one night in the same township. I was coming home and I got caught up in them. In the first, I was getting pushed and I could see the funeral procession around me. I felt I was being controlled. But, with a struggle, I got through it, and about two or three hundred yards further on, I was into another. The two people involved died within about a month of one another. Oh, it's a queer thing.

On another occasion, I was visiting my uncle and it was a moonlight night. I was reasonably young at the time. I spent two or three hours with my uncle and then I headed home about midnight. I walked down through the field – there were no fences like you get nowadays – to the main road. So, at that time of night, I stepped it out, but I noticed an old man walking in front of me on the cart track. I knew who it was, but I kept back a bit and I noticed this other person coming over to meet him from the opposite direction. I said to myself that it was funny that they were on the same side of the track and I wondered what was going to happen as they headed for one another. The two became one. The one absorbed the other. That old man was dead within three weeks.

But, the likes of me, I'm not as mobile as I used to be. I hardly leave the house, and when I do it's in a car, so I haven't experienced anything in the last couple of years or so. I dare say if I was on the move like I was when I was young, the gift would still be there. You don't hear anything about second sight now. It could be because of the rat race, or maybe it's just that nobody takes much notice of it now.

B: Another reason is that the population on the island is getting smaller.

But second sight was common in the Celtic races. Possibly if you told these things to a Lowlander, they would just laugh in your face. Second sight was very, very common on all the islands.

The most famous man to have it on this island was a fellow MacLean. He was known more as a prophet than a seer. Alasdair B. was a policeman in Glasgow and I remember ceilidhing with him one night after he retired back here, and he was talking about this old man. Alasdair said that he and his uncle were collecting tangles on the shore one day and the old man came across and talked to the uncle. He knew the uncle well. And Alasdair said, "I was sitting on a rock a wee bit away, but I was hearing the conversation and all of a sudden he [MacLean] turned to my uncle and he said, 'There's a terrible war coming. I won't see it, but you'll see it, and that young boy there, he'll see it, I can see the blood on him.'" And Alasdair B. was wounded in France. And I believe every word of that story because Alasdair had no reason for telling a lie.

A: No. He wouldn't. Alasdair wouldn't.

B: Alasdair would have been about 13 at the time. I think MacLean died in 1913 or something like that. He was dead before the First World War anyway. He prophesied the Second World War too. He prophesied the fighting in the sky. He could see the blood pouring out of the sky. And he could see people going about with snouts on them like pigs. That was the gas masks he was seeing.

He was a very, very religious man. He was always reading the Bible. He was a very religious man, and yet, he had that gift.

A: Like everything else, it runs in families. *B* there has seen a few instances, as did his folk before him.

B: I remember one story about my grandfather. He was going home across the fields one day and there was a plank across what we called the big burn. And when he got to this plank, his neighbour was standing on it. He knew, of course, that this was a spirit, so he jumped the burn and when he got home, the spirit was standing in the doorway. It was my grandfather that coffined that man.

Then there were lights. People would see ghostly lights. There was an old man I remember, and he had had a brother, and this brother used to visit his granny. He was coming home one night and he fell over a rock and he must have been stunned and he was drowned when the tide came in. They were all out searching for him and they couldn't find him and his brother came home and said, "You don't need to search further, I'll take you to the spot where he is. I've been seeing a light there for the past two years." And he took them down and they found him there.

And another thing. People used to hear the psalms. When there was a funeral, they would take the coffin outside and they would sing a psalm. People would hear the singing before the death took place. A lot of people would hear that that didn't have second sight as such.

Mary Maclean

Eoligarry, Barra

Mary was born in 1938 in the house which is still her home.
Educated locally and in Fort William, she went into domestic
service in Glasgow as a young woman. Although she enjoyed life
in the city, she chose to return to Barra 20 years ago. In a soft,
thoughtful tone, she explained why.

My father and mother were getting old and I felt that I should
come back and help with the croft. I'm very pleased that I did
because I found that when I came back, I listened more to the
stories that I had heard as a child and had disregarded because
there was always tomorrow. And I think that I was very fortunate
to be able to come back and enjoy hearing these stories in the
latter years of my parents' lives. I got that second chance, so that I
sit here now in middle age and feel that I can have a step, a
foothold, in each culture: what I heard from my parents about their
parents and their grandparents, and what I myself knew as a child;
and what I can now see from a sedentary position of how life has
changed in the island, how the young ones have coped with
changes that have come into their ambit.

The stories we heard were usually about families. Stories about
villages being settled, especially after the First World War. That
was when my father got this croft. There was an agitation in years
leading up to that time, when people felt the need to have more
land. This particular village was broken up into 40 crofts and there
was a kind of lottery system and my father got this one. So, we
heard tales of that, and we heard tales of his childhood and

working on this land which he was later to have part of as a croft. We used to hear tales of family trees. You knew who was related. You knew who came on that line and who came on the next line.

We heard tales about how the people were cleared out of their land and it always seemed as if it happened last week because that sense of injustice still burned like a flame on the heather. It was still there. We heard of places that had retained names given to them at those times; of stones thrown down into the shore when houses were knocked down in order that the people wouldn't go back in and shelter. And the places were called after the persons who directed these atrocities. For example: *Clachan Pharry*. Parry was obviously the person in charge. Clachan were the stones from the building thrown into the shore – and they're still there.

There's a place up on the west side, a hill above Cleat, and there's a split up near the top there – a gully, a very narrow gully – and it's called *Scutag Iain Og*. Now, Iain Og was an old, old man who, in an attempt to get away from the ones who were responsible for gathering the people and shipping them off, took his horse and a small cart up there and managed to get right up into the hillside where he wouldn't be found. How he managed to get the cart up, I don't know. But it did happen and the name is still there.

I talk to my grand-nieces and nephews. I tell them little stories – as much to keep them quiet as anything else. [Laughter]. I have them re-enacting little stories and my chairs get laldy of course – they're hills and they're rocks and they're ships, and what not – but sometimes you can get the story across better that way. When we're being terribly proper they're not allowed to play like that – when other folk are around. But when they're down on their own, sometimes we have the MacGregors, sometimes we have Bonnie Prince Charlie and we have him going to Skye here. [Pointing to a chair in the corner]. And they absorb it.

I have no children but I think that in each one of us there is that torch that we want to hand on. And if, like me, you are fortunate enough to be able to borrow the families of all your nieces and nephews, and the parents are generous enough to allow you to have the company of all these wee ones, you feel then that you in turn can pass on something.

I think the factor that has the greatest influence on family life now is the television. I'm sure there are very few houses where there isn't a television in the corner and it brings into your living-room the rest of the world. So children are bound to be conditioned by this knowledge, this awareness of the outside world. They are much more *au fait* with world conditions than we were – although, the island was always a seafaring community and you knew all of the places and you'd heard tales of them. The menfolk would come home – your father, your brothers who were in the merchant navy – and they would talk about these places. And names like Panama Canal were common enough when I was a child. You knew all the sea ports. You knew where the village boys were. So the world was part of the conversation round the fireside. Karachi, Bombay, Valparaiso, Buenos Aires – all these were names you spoke about because members of the family had been there. But the cultures of these places never impinged upon family life as I feel the cultures of the soaps do today. Ramsay Street must have quite an influence on today's child.

A lot has been gained from television because children learn, but perhaps there are things it brings that we could do without in our communities – fashion, a way of looking at life, things which sometimes conflict with the values that we had passed on by our forebears. Perhaps it's a sign of growing old but sometimes I find it difficult to reconcile myself with some of these ideas and some of these things that I see on television.

Mary has written several plays and sketches which have been performed locally. The sketches, she says, "are a bit of fun; just my way of making a comment on things that have happened, things

that relate to island life – new buildings, television crews coming
up, the final results of the television crews' findings."

Before allowing me to switch on the tape recorder, she had
quizzed me on my motives. Was I, she wanted to know, another of
those people who simply want to "tear the islands apart?"

Well, journalists come in and they have preconceived notions of
island life. And I try to think that perhaps if I went to Hawaii or
somewhere I'd have ideas about what I expected and that if I found
the people had moved forward and were no longer in the 17th
century, I might be disappointed because they were spoiling my
idea of what my television documentary was to be about.

Instead of waiting until they get here, they seem to have their
colours all painted in before they come. And when we don't fit
into their scheme, they're a bit taken aback. When they're talking
about islanders, they're not talking about insular people. They are
talking about people who have travelled the world over and have
brought back to their families their idea of the outside world. We
are not still in the 17th century, we are as forward looking as these
people who are behind the cameras.

One particular television crew focused to a degree that seemed
a little in excess on drinking habits. I am sure that in every place
you'll find a few who over-indulge. We don't any more than
anywhere else. The island may have come to the forefront of
publicity through Compton Mackenzie's film *Whisky Galore* – but
that was only a title. You can't come and expect to find the party of
the Politician still going on.

But I think that the Gaelic programmes have done a lot to dispel
some of the impressions created by these people.

Islanders are survivors. We have lived through hard times and
good times. And I think that we realise we are a family and how
much we need each other, and it gives you a closeness. When
good times come, we rejoice for our neighbours – as they do for
us. When tragedy comes, as a seafaring people we sorrow because

we know that only by the turn of the coin is it someone else, and not you, today. It might be you tomorrow.

When our young folk go away, that thread of affection that you have for the island community doesn't break. It follows them. Their fortunes when they go to the mainland are of interest to us all. And if they fall on hard times, in some way or another it awakens in us feelings of sympathy for them, for they are ours – no matter who they are, they are still islanders. And if they do well and they are successful, we are proud for them. We are happy that they have achieved and that they are ambassadors for the island. We never release them even if perchance they should forget the island for a while. The island doesn't forget them. The island holds on like a mother and they never lose their spot in the affections of the island.

I think that's possibly how I would describe islanders. We all belong. We all need one another. We don't live in one another's pockets but help, a soul to talk to, is never more than a 'phone call away if sorrow should come.

Mary married late in life. She met her husband James, a Gaelic-speaking Canadian of Barra descent, while on holiday in Cape Breton. He moved to Barra and the couple were married in 1981. Sadly, James died five years later.

Today, with her brother, Mary still runs the family croft. I was curious to know what she enjoys about outdoor life.

Oh, just working and [pause] being able to stand in the fields without having to give an excuse and look up at the hill above the house that I've seen since childhood. There's an old dun up there, an old fort. Our house is named Dunscurrival because the stones that built it were taken out of there.

When I was a child up there on the hill, I would watch the sun going down behind the dun. That was always a picture I carried with me when I was away from home. And to work now in the fields and to be able to lean on the fork for a minute to look at it...

And it's there. And suddenly I'm no longer a middle-aged, grey-haired lady. I am a child of six. Climbing up there. I am a young teenager thinking of romance. I am a young woman in my 20s and 30s, happy to be coming home and knowing that it's going to be there. And then I'm me, just now, happy to see the family growing up knowing that it's there – something so permanent. The magic of it is still there. I don't know what it is...

When you were coming home on holiday, you'd come into the village and your heart would beat that little bit faster when you saw the house. And then, after you'd had your tea, you'd go away up to gather the cows – really just so that you'd have a chance to go up there.

You felt secure up there, knowing that everything was alright because those you loved were down here. They had told you all the stories; and the hill was always part of life some way. I have been up there since my parents died and I can sit and look down on the house and, just for a minute, time stops and I'm once again a carefree child. Home is there – a safe haven. My father and mother are there, and brothers and sisters: everything that made it possible for me to be carefree and secure.

I love all the birds, but you'll never believe what my favourite is. The corncrake. She comes in summer; we've got them all round here. And it's evocative of childhood when it seemed to me that the whole wide world was asleep and I was standing on a box at the skylight being sure that they were saying, "*Mary*. Come out. Come out." Me – all of six or seven – and the corncrakes having this conversation.

They were always part of younger life. Childhood. And teenage years. And boyfriends. And coming home in summer. And children coming in the family – my brother getting married and my sister getting married and coming home with their babies. And corncrakes. And some way or another the magic of life is there. You wanted some way to encapsulate the moment for the family and [extending cupped hands] say, "Here. Keep that forever."

And now, I don't know what it is but there's something new. I didn't feel it before because I was young. But now, and I've only